SECOND EDITION

VOLUME THREE

Leo Dillon and Diane Dillon to Eloise Greenfield

Favorite Children's
AUTHORS *and* ILLUSTRATORS

E. Russell Primm III, Editor in Chief

PO Box 326, Chanhassen, MN 55317-0326
800/599-READ
http://www.childsworld.com

A Note to Our Readers:

The publication dates listed in each author's or illustrator's selected bibliography represent the date of first publication in the United States.

The editors have listed literary awards that were announced prior to August 2006.

Every effort has been made to contact copyright holders of material included in this reference work. If any errors or omissions have occurred, corrections will be made in future editions.

Photographs: 12—Louise Erdrich / Hyperion; 16, 88, 136—Scholastic; 20—Lois Duncan; 24—Estate of Roger Duvoisin; 28, 36, 84—Harcourt; 32—Lauren Wojtyla / HarperCollins; 40, 72—HarperCollins; 44—de Grummond Collection, University of Southern Mississippi; 48—Roddy McDowell; 52—Mark Lennihan / AP Photo; 56—Colin McPherson / Corbis; 64—Hyperion; 68—Becky Mojica / HarperCollins; 76—Henry Holt; 80—Houghton Mifflin / Kerlan Collection, University of Minnesota; 92—Carlo Ontal / Houghton Mifflin; 96—Kerlan Collection, University of Minnesota; 100—Penguin Putnam; 104—The Chicken House; 108—Philadelphia Museum of Art; 112—Whittlesey House / Kerlan Collection, University of Minnesota; 116—Merry Scully / HarperCollins; 120—Children's Book Press; 124—Ellen Young Photography / Harper-Collins; 128—Bob Stern / The Republican / AP Photo; 132—Kent Antcliffe / Harcourt; 140—Tim Keating / Random House; 144—Simon & Schuster; 148—Hulton-Deutsch Collection / Corbis.

An Editorial Directions book

Library of Congress Cataloging-in-Publication Data

Favorite children's authors and illustrators / E. Russell Primm III, editor-in-chief. — 2nd ed.
   v. cm.
  Includes bibliographical references and index.
  Contents: v. 1. Verna Aardema to Ashley Bryan.
  ISBN-13: 978-1-59187-057-9 (v.1 : alk. paper)
  ISBN-10: 1-59187-057-7 (v. 1 : alk. paper)
  ISBN-13: 978-1-59187-058-6 (v. 2 : alk. paper)
  ISBN-10: 1-59187-058-5 (v. 2 : alk. paper)
  ISBN-13: 978-1-59187-059-3 (v. 3 : alk. paper)
  ISBN-10: 1-59187-059-3 (v. 3 : alk. paper)
  ISBN-13: 978-1-59187-060-9 (v. 4 : alk. paper)
  ISBN-10: 1-59187-060-7 (v. 4 : alk. paper)
  ISBN-13: 978-1-59187-061-6 (v. 5 : alk. paper)
  ISBN-10: 1-59187-061-5 (v. 5 : alk. paper)
  ISBN-13: 978-1-59187-062-3 (v. 6 : alk. paper)
  ISBN-10: 1-59187-062-3 (v. 6 : alk. paper)
  ISBN-13: 978-1-59187-063-0 (v. 7 : alk. paper)
  ISBN-10: 1-59187-063-1 (v. 7 : alk. paper)
  ISBN-13: 978-1-59187-064-7 (v. 8 : alk. paper)
  ISBN-10: 1-59187-064-X (v. 8 : alk. paper)
  1. Children's literature—Bio-bibliography—Dictionaries—Juvenile literature. 2. Young adult literature Bio-bibliography—Dictionaries—Juvenile literature. 3. Illustrators—Biography—Dictionaries—Juvenile literature. 4. Children—Books and reading—Dictionaries—Juvenile literature. 5. Young Adults—Books and reading—Dictionaries—Juvenile literature. I. Primm, E. Russell, 1958–
  PN1009.A1F38 2007
  809'.8928203—dc22
  [B]   2006011358

T ABLE OF CONTENTS

MAJOR CHILDREN'S AUTHOR AND ILLUSTRATOR LITERARY AWARDS

THE AMERICAN BOOK AWARDS

Awarded from 1980 to 1983 in place of the National Book Award to give national recognition to achievement in several categories of children's literature

THE BOSTON GLOBE–HORN BOOK AWARDS

Established in 1967 by Horn Book *magazine and the* Boston Globe *newspaper to honor the year's best fiction, poetry, nonfiction, and picture books for children*

THE CALDECOTT MEDAL

Established in 1938 and presented by the Association for Library Service to Children division of the American Library Association to illustrators for the most distinguished picture book for children from the preceding year

THE CARNEGIE MEDAL

Established in 1936 and presented by the British Library Association for an outstanding book for children written in English

THE CARTER G. WOODSON BOOK AWARDS

Established in 1974 and presented by the National Council for the Social Studies for the most distinguished social science books appropriate for young readers that depict ethnicity in the United States

THE CORETTA SCOTT KING AWARDS

Established in 1970 in connection with the American Library Association to honor African American authors and illustrators whose books are deemed outstanding, educational, and inspirational

THE HANS CHRISTIAN ANDERSEN MEDAL

Established in 1956 by the International Board on Books for Young People to honor an author or illustrator, living at the time of nomination, whose complete works have made a lasting contribution to children's literature

THE KATE GREENAWAY MEDAL

Established by the Youth Libraries Group of the British Library Association in 1956 to honor illustrators of children's books published in the United Kingdom

THE LAURA INGALLS WILDER AWARD

Established by the Association for Library Service to Children division of the American Library Association in 1954 to honor an author or illustrator whose books, published in the United States, have made a substantial and lasting contribution to children's literature

THE MICHAEL L. PRINTZ AWARD

Established by the Young Adult Library Services division of the American Library Association in 2000 to honor literary excellence in young adult literature (fiction, nonfiction, poetry, or anthology)

THE NATIONAL BOOK AWARDS

Established in 1950 to give national recognition to achievement in fiction, nonfiction, poetry, and young people's literature

THE NEWBERY MEDAL

Established in 1922 and presented by the Association for Library Service to Children division of the American Library Association for the most distinguished contribution to children's literature in the preceding year

THE ORBIS PICTUS AWARD FOR OUTSTANDING NONFICTION

Established in 1990 by the National Council of Teachers of English to honor an outstanding informational book published in the preceding year

THE PURA BELPRÉ AWARD

Established in 1996 and cosponsored by the Association for Library Service to Children division of the American Library Association and the National Association to Promote Library Services to the Spanish Speaking to recognize a writer and illustrator of Latino or Latina background whose works affirm and celebrate the Latino experience

THE SCOTT O'DELL AWARD

Established in 1982 and presented by the O'Dell Award Committee to an American author who writes an outstanding tale of historical fiction for children or young adults that takes place in the New World

Leo Dillon
Diane Dillon

Born: March 2, 1933 (Leo)
Born: March 13, 1933 (Diane)

Leo and Diane Dillon have been illustrating books together for more than forty years. They have illustrated more than fifty children's books for other authors including *Why Mosquitoes Buzz in People's Ears; Ashanti to Zulu: African Traditions;* and *Aïda.* The Dillons have also created illustrations for posters, advertisements, and album covers.

Leo and Diane were both born in 1933—in different parts of

the country. Diane was born on March 13 in Glendale, California. Leo was born on March 2 in Brooklyn, New York.

Leo and Diane met in 1953 as students at the Parsons School of Design in New York City. They had seen each other's art

DIANE DILLON CREATED A STAINED GLASS CEILING THAT WAS INSTALLED IN THE EAGLE GALLERY IN NEW YORK CITY.

before they actually met. After they met, they competed to see who was the better artist.

The Dillons began working together shortly after they married in 1957. They established their own company called Studio 2. The first children's book they illustrated was *Hakon of Rogen's Saga*. The book, written by Erik C. Haugaard, was published in 1963.

The Dillons have illustrated books by many other children's authors. Their work has won

A Selected Bibliography of the Dillons' Work

Earth Mother (2005)

The People Could Fly: The Picture Book (2004)

One Winter's Night (2003)

Rap a Tap Tap Here's Bojangles—Think of That! (2002)

The Girl Who Spun Gold (2000)

Her Stories: African American Folktales, Fairy Tales, and True Tales (1995)

Switch on the Night (1993)

Aïda (1991)

The Tale of the Mandarin Ducks (1989)

The People Could Fly: American Black Folktales (1985)

Who's in Rabbit's House? A Masai Tale (1977)

Ashanti to Zulu: African Traditions (1976)

The Hundred Penny Box (1975)

Song of the Boat (1975)

Why Mosquitoes Buzz in People's Ears (1975)

The Ring in the Prairie: A Shawnee Legend (1970)

Hakon of Rogen's Saga (1963)

The Dillons' Major Literary Awards

2005 Coretta Scott King Illustrator Honor Book
The People Could Fly: The Picture Book

2003 Coretta Scott King Illustrator Honor Book
Rap a Tap Tap: Here's Bojangles—Think of That!

1996 Coretta Scott King Illustrator Honor Book
Her Stories: African American Folktales, Fairy Tales, and True Tales

1991 Boston Globe-Horn Book Picture Book Award
The Tale of the Mandarin Ducks

1991 Coretta Scott King Illustrator Award
Aïda

1986 Coretta Scott King Illustrator Honor Book
The People Could Fly: American Black Folktales

1977 Boston Globe-Horn Book Picture Book Honor Book
1977 Caldecott Medal
Ashanti to Zulu: African Traditions

1976 Boston Globe-Horn Book Picture Book Honor Book
Song of the Boat

1976 Caldecott Medal
Why Mosquitoes Buzz in People's Ears

1975 Boston Globe-Horn Book Fiction Honor Book
The Hundred Penny Box

> *"Together we are able to create art that we would not be able to do individually."*
> —Leo and Diane Dillon

them many awards, including the Caldecott Medal and the Coretta Scott King Illustrator Award. The Dillons were the first illustrators to win the Caldecott Medal two years in a row—in 1976 and in 1977.

Leo and Diane Dillon have a collaborative approach to their work. Leo might work on a sketch and then pass it to Diane. Then she might add something and pass it back to Leo. When the illustration is complete, it is a combination of their ideas. The Dillons refer to this process as "the third artist" because the final work is something they probably couldn't have created on their own. "At the point we hit the 'third artist' concept, it helped us a lot, because we could look at ourselves as an artist rather than two individuals," Diane Dillon explains.

The Dillons' illustrations are often a combination of art techniques. They sometimes have to learn new tech-

> *"Art in its many forms has survived to inform us of lives long gone. Art inspires, lifts our spirits, and brings beauty to our lives. We wish to pay homage to it and the people that created it."*
> —Leo and Diane Dillon

LEO DILLON WAS THE FIRST AFRICAN AMERICAN TO WIN THE CALDECOTT MEDAL. HE WON THE MEDAL WITH DIANE IN 1976 FOR THEIR ILLUSTRATIONS IN *WHY MOSQUITOES BUZZ IN PEOPLE'S EARS*.

niques for a book. Other times, they invent their own. "We take great pride in illustration and the fact that we are illustrators," Diane Dillon says. "We've never thought there is a difference between 'fine art' and illustration other than good art or bad art."

The Dillons continue to create illustrations for children's books. They have a son and live in New York City.

 ❦

WHERE TO FIND OUT MORE ABOUT LEO AND DIANE DILLON

BOOKS

McElmeel, Sharron L. *100 Most Popular Picture Book Authors and Illustrators: Biographical Sketches and Bibliographies*. Englewood, Colo.: Libraries Unlimited, 2000.

Silvey, Anita, ed. *The Essential Guide to Children's Books and Their Creators*. Boston: Houghton Mifflin Company, 2002.

WEB SITES

KIDSREADS.COM
http://www.kidsreads.com/authors/au-dillon-leo-diane.asp
To read a biographical sketch of Leo and Diane Dillon

SCHOLASTIC AUTHORS ONLINE
http://www2.scholastic.com/teachers/authorsandbooks/authorstudies/ authorhome.jhtml?authorID=210&collateralID=5146&displayName=Biography
To read a biographical sketch of Leo and Diane Dillon

———

THE DILLONS' SON, LIONEL JOHN DILLON III, IS A PAINTER, SCULPTOR, AND JEWELRY CRAFTSPERSON. HE HAS ALSO WORKED WITH HIS PARENTS ON THE ILLUSTRATIONS FOR SEVERAL BOOKS.

Michael Dorris

Born: January 30, 1945
Died: April 11, 1997

Michael Dorris was part Modoc Indian. He did many kinds of work—teaching, research, and writing nonfiction and fiction for adults and children. His concern for Native Americans was part of almost everything he did during his life.

Michael Dorris was born on January 30, 1945, in Louisville, Kentucky. His father was killed in World War II (1938–1945), and Michael lived with his mother, grandmother, and aunt, except for a little time he spent on a reservation in Montana.

After high school, Dorris went to Georgetown University in Washington, D.C. Then he got a graduate degree in anthropology at Yale University in New Haven, Connecticut. Part of Dorris's research involved living in a fishing village in Alaska.

———

MICHAEL DORRIS GOT THE IDEA FOR HIS FIRST YOUNG-ADULT NOVEL, *MORNING GIRL,* WHEN HE STARTED WONDERING ABOUT A YOUNG TAINO GIRL MENTIONED IN AN ENTRY IN CHRISTOPHER COLUMBUS'S DIARY.

In Alaska, Dorris adopted a three-year-old Sioux boy named Abel. He became one of the first unmarried men in the United States to adopt a child. Eventually Dorris adopted two other American Indian children.

> *"When I was growing up . . . I rarely encountered Native American fictional characters with whom I could identify. The native peoples I read about in books always seemed to be performing rather dull crafts—sort of like earnest Boy Scouts—or riding around on ponies bareback, whooping it up."*

In 1979, Dorris started a department dedicated to Native American studies at Dartmouth University in Hanover, New Hampshire. At Dartmouth, he met Louise Erdrich, a student who was also part American Indian and interested in writing. The two married in 1981. Michael Dorris and Louise Erdrich became one of the best-known literary couples in the United States.

Erdrich's fiction, starting with *Love Medicine* in 1985, concerned Native Americans. Dorris also published a novel, but it was his nonfiction book *The Broken Cord* that became a bestseller. In *The Broken Cord,* Dorris wrote about the struggle to help his adopted son, Abel, who suffered from fetal alcohol syndrome (FAS). FAS is a combination of birth defects that tend to occur in babies whose mothers drink large amounts of alcohol during pregnancy. *The Broken Cord* informed people

DORRIS OPPOSED USING AMERICAN INDIAN NAMES FOR PRODUCTS AND SPORTS TEAMS. WHEN HE WAS AT DARTMOUTH UNIVERSITY, HE SPENT FIFTEEN YEARS TRYING TO GET THE DARTMOUTH INDIANS TO CHANGE THEIR NAME. TODAY, THE TEAM IS KNOWN AS THE BIG GREEN.

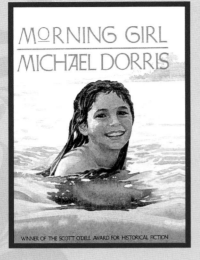

WINNER OF THE SCOTT O'DELL AWARD FOR HISTORICAL FICTION

A Selected Bibliography of Dorris's Work

The Window (1997)

Sees Behind Trees (1996)

Guests (1994)

Morning Girl (1992)

Dorris's Major Literary Awards

1993 Scott O'Dell Award
  Morning Girl

about the plight of children with FAS and the dangers of drinking during pregnancy.

Dorris kept writing novels and short stories for adults. He also began to write for young people. Dorris's first children's book, *Morning Girl,* was published in 1992—500 years after Christopher Columbus discovered America. This book of historical fiction tells about the lives of a young brother and sister who are Taino Indians— the first people that Columbus met in the Americas.

More novels followed. *Guests* is about an Indian boy who is unhappy that his father has invited European colonists to their harvest feast. In *Sees Behind Trees,* a Native American boy wants to become a hunter but has to learn to overcome his nearsightedness.

In spite of his success, Michael Dorris suffered from depression. On April 11, 1997, he took his own life in Concord, New Hampshire. His young-adult book *The Window* was published in 1997 after his death.

> *"There are many things that Indian people are not:. . . .They are not represented by the stereotypes of Hollywood or most fiction; they are not people without history, languages, literatures, sciences, and arts; they are not vanished, and are not vanishing."*

WHERE TO FIND OUT MORE ABOUT MICHAEL DORRIS

BOOKS

Holtze, Sally Holmes, ed. *Seventh Book of Junior Authors & Illustrators.* New York: H. W. Wilson Company, 1996.

Weil, Ann. *Michael Dorris.* Austin, Texas: Raintree/Steck-Vaughn, 1997.

WEB SITES

E MUSEUM: MICHAEL DORRIS
http://emuseum.mnsu.edu/information/biography/abcde/dorris_michael.html
To read a brief biographical sketch of Michael Dorris

SCHOLASTIC AUTHORS ONLINE
http://books.scholastic.com/teachers/authorsandbooks/authorstudies/authorhome.
jsp?authorID=30&collateralID=5150&displayName=Biography
For an autobiographical sketch by Michael Dorris, a booklist,
and a transcript an interview

DORRIS'S FAVORITE AUTHOR AS A CHILD WAS HIS MOTHER. SHE "MADE UP NEW STORIES EVERY NIGHT. NONE OF THEM WERE WRITTEN DOWN BUT ALL OF THEM WERE MAGICAL AND SPECIAL BECAUSE THEY WERE JUST FOR ME," DORRIS SAID.

Arthur Dorros

Born: May 19, 1950

Many authors write about experiences they have had themselves. Author and illustrator Arthur Dorros does exactly that in his books. For example, Dorros lived in South America for a year and used his experience to write *Tonight Is Carnaval,* a story about a South American family getting ready to celebrate Carnaval.

Arthur Dorros speaks English and Spanish and writes in both

languages. He wants children in the United States to know about life in other countries. One of Dorros's books, *This Is My House,* shows the different types of houses that children live in all over the world. On each page the words "This is my house" are written in the language spoken in the country featured.

Another of Arthur Dorros's books mixes Spanish phrases with an English text. *Abuela,*

WHEN HE WAS FOUR YEARS OLD, ARTHUR DORROS SAT ON THE TAIL OF A TEN-FOOT ALLIGATOR. HE USED THIS EXPERIENCE TO WRITE HIS SECOND BOOK, *ALLIGATOR SHOES.*

which means "grandmother" in Spanish, is the story of a girl named Rosalba who dreams that she and her grandmother fly together over New York City. Another book, *Isla,* continues the story of Rosalba and Abuela. The grandmother and granddaughter visit the Caribbean island where Abuela grew up. Dorros drew on his close relationship with his own grandmother to write these stories.

Because he loves nature, Dorros also writes and illustrates nonfiction science books for

> "I believe you can achieve what you want, if you're willing to work at it, and have fun at the same time."

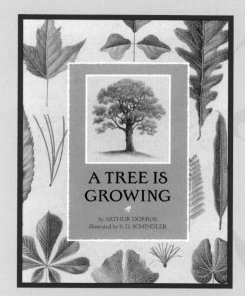

A Selected Bibliography of Dorros's Work

Julio's Magic (2005)
Under the Sun (2004)
City Chicken (2002)
When the Pigs Took Over (2002)
The Fungus That Ate My School (2000)
Ten Go Tango (2000)
A Tree Is Growing (1997)
Isla (1995)
Elephant Families (1994)
Radio Man=Don Radio: A Story in English and Spanish (1993)
This Is My House (1992)
Abuela (1991)
Animal Tracks (1991)
Follow the Water from Brook to Ocean (1991)
Tonight Is Carnaval (1991)
Rain Forest Secrets (1990)
Feel the Wind (1989)
Ant Cities (1987)
What Makes Day and Night (Illustrations only, 1986)
Charlie's House (Illustrations only, 1983)
Alligator Shoes (1982)
Pretzels (1981)

Dorros's Major Literary Awards

1998 Orbis Pictus Honor Book
  A Tree Is Growing

young children. He has written books about ants, elephants, water, and the wind. The National Science Teachers Association selected three of his books—*Ant Cities, Feel the Wind,* and *Rain Forest Secrets*—as outstanding science books. Another book, *A Tree Is Growing,* won an award from the American Horticultural Society in 1998.

> *"I wasn't born an author. I had to learn . . . [that you] have to keep on trying and don't let anyone make you stop."*

Born on May 19, 1950, Arthur Dorros grew up in Washington, D.C. He loved to read and draw when he was young. He says his father was a great storyteller. Arthur's mother kept bottles of tempera paint and other art supplies on hand for him.

In high school, Arthur became hooked on drawing when he had to draw amoebas and other creatures as part of his biology assignments. Later, he became hooked on telling stories to children in his neighborhood. He finally put the two things he enjoyed the most—storytelling and drawing—together. He created his first picture book, *Pretzels,* when he was twenty-nine.

Before he became a published writer, Arthur Dorros had many other jobs. He was a carpenter, an elementary school teacher, a farm-

ARTHUR DORROS LOVED DRAWING WHEN HE WAS A CHILD, BUT GAVE IT UP IN FIFTH GRADE BECAUSE HE THOUGHT HE WAS NOT VERY GOOD! NOW HE TELLS CHILDREN TO KEEP TRYING THINGS EVEN IF THEY MAKE A MISTAKE.

worker, and a photographer. He enjoys meeting people and learning about them. These different jobs helped him prepare for his career as a writer. He thinks that a good writer or illustrator is like a detective. A detective looks for clues to solve a mystery; a writer looks for clues to tell a good story.

❦

WHERE TO FIND OUT MORE ABOUT ARTHUR DORROS

BOOKS

Holtze, Sally Holmes, ed. *Seventh Book of Junior Authors & Illustrators.* New York: H. W. Wilson Company, 1996.

Something about the Author. Vol. 122. Detroit: Gale Research, 2001.

WEB SITES

ARTHUR DORROS HOME PAGE
http://www.arthurdorros.com/
To read an autobiographical account by Arthur Dorros and information about his books

READING PLANET
http://www.rif.org/readingplanet/bookzone/content/dorros.mspx
For an interview with the author

DORROS HAS LIVED IN MANY PLACES IN THE UNITED STATES, FROM ONE COAST TO THE OTHER. HE WAS BORN IN WASHINGTON, D.C., AND GRADUATED FROM THE UNIVERSITY OF WISCONSIN. NOW HE LIVES ON THE WEST COAST, IN SEATTLE, WASHINGTON.

Lois Duncan

Born: April 28, 1934

Even as a young child, Lois Duncan knew she wanted to be a writer. When she was just ten years old, Lois began sending stories to magazines. At the age of thirteen, she sold her first story for twenty-five dollars! In 1958, she wrote her first full-length novel, *Debutante Hill.* Since then, Lois has penned more than forty books.

Some of Duncan's best-loved novels are eerie mysteries for young adults. Several of Duncan's chilling stories have inspired made-for-TV

movies and feature films. *Summer of Fear, Killing Mr. Griffin,* and *Don't Look Behind You* were made into television movies. *I Know What You Did Last Summer* was released as a feature film in 1997.

Lois Duncan was born in Philadelphia, Pennsylvania, on April 28, 1934. Her parents, Joseph and Lois Steinmetz, were magazine photographers. They both encouraged Lois's love of storytelling.

LOIS DUNCAN HATED THE MOVIE VERSION OF *I KNOW WHAT YOU DID LAST SUMMER.* SHE FELT THAT IT WAS MUCH TOO VIOLENT.

When Lois was just a toddler, her
parents wrote down and saved the
stories she made up for them. Lois and
her parents moved to Sarasota, Florida,
when her brother, Billy, was born.

> "*Writing gives you the power to
> create whole worlds and make
> everything in them happen the
> way you want it to.*"

Growing up, Lois was a shy book-
worm who wore braces and eyeglasses. To help her through her teen
years, Lois poured her thoughts and feelings into stories. When she
wasn't given a part in the school play, for example, she wrote a story in
which she won the starring role.

As an adult, Duncan found that she could earn a living by writing.
After her first marriage ended in 1961, she moved with her three small
children to Albuquerque, New Mexico, to be near her brother. Duncan
supported her family by writing magazine articles. Once she remarried,
however, she turned her attention to the kind of writing she loved best:
fiction for young adults.

In 1966, Duncan wrote *Ransom,* her first young-adult suspense novel.
Ransom was a hit with teens who loved spine-tingling mysteries. It was also
a runner-up for the Edgar Allan Poe Award, a prize given for outstanding
mystery writing. Since then, each novel Duncan writes earns her new fans.
Teens love her stories' supernatural twists and realistic teenage characters.

OVER THE YEARS, LOIS DUNCAN HAS RECEIVED MANY AWARDS FOR HER
WRITING. IN 1992, SHE WON THE MARGARET E. EDWARDS AWARD FOR
OUTSTANDING TEEN FICTION.

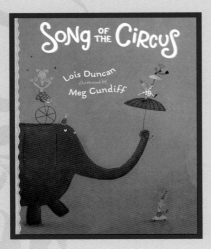

A Selected Bibliography of Duncan's Work

Song of the Circus (2002)

I Walk at Night (2000)

The Longest Hair in the World (1999)

Gallows Hill (1997)

The Magic of Spider Woman (1996)

Who Killed My Daughter? (1992)

The Birthday Moon (1989)

Don't Look Behind You (1989)

They Never Came Home (1989)

The Twisted Window (1987)

Locked in Time (1985)

The Third Eye (1984)

The Terrible Tales of Happy Days School (1983)

Chapters: My Growth As a Writer (1982)

Stranger with My Face (1981)

Daughters of Eve (1979)

Killing Mr. Griffin (1978)

Summer of Fear (1976)

Down a Dark Hall (1974)

I Know What You Did Last Summer (1973)

A Gift of Magic (1971)

Hotel for Dogs (1971)

Peggy (1970)

Ransom (1966)

Season of the Two-Heart (1964)

Game of Danger (1962)

Debutante Hill (1958)

Lois Duncan has never forgotten the advice of a friend who told her to write about what she knows. Many of her books are set in the Southwest or near the ocean—places where Duncan has lived. Over the years, Duncan has tried different styles of writing. She has written nonfiction books for both adults and young adults. She wrote picture books for her grandchildren to enjoy. She has also written books of poetry. In 1982, Duncan even published her autobiography.

> *"Sometimes I feel that I am two people in one, with a part of me living each experience and another part observing."*

In 1989, personal tragedy struck: Duncan's eighteen-year-old daughter, Kaitlyn, was shot to death while driving. Officials determined that the killing was a random shooting, but Duncan was unconvinced. In 1992, Duncan wrote the book *Who Killed My Daughter?* She hopes that the book might encourage someone to provide information to help find her daughter's killer. "It's not a matter of revenge. It's a matter of Kait being worth the truth," she explains.

Since the loss of her daughter, Duncan has written several books. She continues to tell fascinating stories for people of all ages. Fans of Duncan's work can count on more books in the future. For this award-winning author, writing is like breathing.

WHERE TO FIND OUT MORE ABOUT LOIS DUNCAN

BOOKS

Duncan, Lois. *Chapters: My Growth As a Writer.* Boston: Little, Brown, 1982.

Kies, Cosette. *Presenting Lois Duncan.* New York: Twayne Publishers, 1993.

WEB SITES

LOIS DUNCAN HOME PAGE
http://loisduncan.arquettes.com
To read a booklist and a letter from Lois Duncan to her fans

RANDOM HOUSE AUTHORS/ILLUSTRATORS
http://www.randomhouse.com/author/results.pperl?authorid=7580
To read a biographical account of Lois Duncan

LOIS DUNCAN OFTEN CREATES CHARACTERS BASED ON PEOPLE SHE KNOWS. IN FACT, SOME OF HER CHARACTERS IN PAST BOOKS WERE BASED ON HER CHILDREN.

Roger Duvoisin

Born: August 28, 1904
Died: June 30, 1980

Roger Duvoisin illustrated more than 140 picture books for children. He was also the author of more than forty of these books, creating unforgettable characters such as Petunia the Goose. Duvoisin is especially remembered for illustrating the Happy Lion stories, written by his wife, Louise Fatio.

Roger Antoine Duvoisin was born in Geneva, Switzerland, in 1904. As a child, he loved reading. He also liked comic books, although his father insisted they were junk and tried to keep him away from them. Roger loved animals, too, and often went to zoos and circuses to draw the

> *"I love the lively curiosity children show toward their surroundings. . . . Adults often lose this refreshing freedom and curiosity as they form set, conventional opinions about their world."*

DUVOISIN ILLUSTRATED SEVERAL COVERS OF THE *NEW YORKER* MAGAZINE. HE ALSO DESIGNED GREETING CARDS FOR THE UNITED NATIONS CHILDREN'S FUND (UNICEF).

animals there. He spent time around farm animals during summer vacations in the French countryside.

Duvoisin studied art and design in Geneva, earning a teaching diploma in 1923. After graduation, he worked as a manager at a pottery-making company in Ferney-Voltaire, a French town near Geneva. In 1925, he married Louise Fatio, who was also a native of Switzerland. They had two sons, Roger and Jacques.

Duvoisin designed scenery for the Geneva Opera and other stage shows in the mid-1920s. He eventually settled into a career as a textile designer. In 1927, he was offered a job designing fabric for H. R.

A Selected Bibliography of Duvoisin's Work

The Happy Lioness (Illustrations only, 1980)
Petunia's Treasure (1975)
Jasmine (1973)
Hector Penguin (Illustrations only, 1973)
The Crocodile in the Tree (1972)
The Beaver Pond (Illustrations only, 1970)
The World in the Candy Egg (Illustrations only, 1967)
The Happy Lion and the Bear (Illustrations only, 1964)
Veronica (1961)
The Happy Lion in Africa (Illustrations only, 1955)
The Happy Lion (Illustrations only, 1954)
Petunia (1950)
White Snow, Bright Snow (Illustrations only, 1947)
The Life and Adventures of Robinson Crusoe (Illustrations only, 1946)
A Child's Garden of Verses (Illustrations only, 1944)
Mother Goose: A Comprehensive Collection of the Rhymes (Illustrations only, 1936)
Donkey-Donkey: The Troubles of a Silly Little Donkey (1933)
A Little Boy Was Drawing (1932)

Duvoisin's Major Literary Awards

1966 Caldecott Honor Book
  Hide and Seek Fog
1948 Caldecott Medal
  White Snow, Bright Snow

> *"It is good to observe that children are now . . . taken more seriously. Because of this, making books for children is a more captivating form of art for the writer and illustrator."*

Mallinson, a silk company in New York City, so the Duvoisins moved to the United States.

One day, Duvoisin noticed his four-year-old son, Roger, drawing pictures for a story. Duvoisin decided to add text and complete the book. He then brought it to work and showed it to the son of the company's president, who in turn showed it to famous publisher Charles Scribner. Scribner published the book, *A Little Boy Was Drawing*, in 1932.

H. R. Mallinson closed in 1931, so Duvoisin worked as a freelance illustrator for magazines and advertising agencies. Meanwhile, he wrote *Donkey-Donkey: The Troubles of a Silly Little Donkey*. This story of an insecure donkey was a great success, remaining popular for decades. Soon, Duvoisin was busy illustrating books by other authors.

In 1939, the Duvoisins moved to a farm in Gladstone, New Jersey. Now surrounded by farm and woodland animals, Duvoisin created some of his best-known characters. They include Petunia, the proud and silly goose; Jasmine, the cow; and Veronica, the hippopotamus. With their human quirks and shortcomings, the animals are both understandable and endearing to young readers.

DUVOISIN HAD AN EARLY INTEREST IN A MUSIC CAREER. BUT HIS FATHER, AN ARCHITECT, URGED HIM TO STUDY ART AND DESIGN INSTEAD.

As Duvoisin worked on his books, his wife gathered ideas for books of her own. In the 1950s, the two embarked on a long and successful collaboration, with Fatio as author and Duvoisin as illustrator. Their most memorable creation is the Happy Lion series. Fatio, on a trip to France, had read a newspaper article about a friendly lion who escaped from a zoo. Building on that idea, the couple produced ten Happy Lion stories, all noted for their themes of warmth, friendship, and kindness.

Duvoisin died in Morristown, New Jersey, two months before his seventy-sixth birthday.

∾

WHERE TO FIND OUT MORE ABOUT ROGER DUVOISIN

BOOKS

Greene, Ellin, and Dorothy Hoogland Verkerk. *Roger Duvoisin: The Art of the Children's Book.* New Brunswick, N.J.: Rutgers, 1989.

Silvey, Anita, ed. *The Essential Guide to Children's Books and Their Creators.* Boston: Houghton Mifflin Company, 2002.

Sutherland, Zena. *Children & Books.* 9th ed. Boston: Allyn & Bacon, 1997.

WEB SITES

BOOK LOON KIDS REVIEWS
http://www.bookloons.com/cgi-bin/Reviews.asp?genre=Kids&bookid=4618
To read reviews of *Petunia's Christmas* and *Veronica*

CHILDREN'S LITERATURE NETWORK
http://www.childrensliteraturenetwork.org/brthpage/08aug/8-28duvoisin.html
To read a biography of the author-illustrator

DUVOISIN ILLUSTRATED MORE THAN A DOZEN BOOKS WRITTEN BY ALVIN TRESSELT. THEIR HIGHLY ACCLAIMED *WHITE SNOW, BRIGHT SNOW* CAPTURES THE MAGIC AND FUN OF A SNOWFALL.

Edward Eager

Born: 1911
Died: October 23, 1964

Edward Eager loved writing about "daily magic." That's the kind of magic that happens to ordinary people as they go about their daily lives. Young people can't get enough of Eager's brand of magic. His fantasy novels for children have been popular for decades.

Edward McMaken Eager was born in 1911 in Toledo, Ohio. He and his family often spent summers in rural Indiana. The Eagers also traveled

frequently, and Edward visited Oregon, California, Australia, and other places.

Edward loved to read, and L. Frank Baum's *The Wizard of Oz* was one of his favorite stories. Even as a child, he knew he wanted to be an author. A friend commented, "He did nothing but study when he was a child, mostly how to write."

EAGER USED HIS HOMETOWN OF TOLEDO, OHIO, AS THE SETTING FOR HIS 1954 NOVEL *HALF MAGIC*.

Edward attended high school at the Tome School in Towson, Maryland. After graduation in the early 1930s, he went to Harvard University in Cambridge, Massachusetts. There he began writing plays for student productions. His play *Pudding Full of Plums* was such a great success that he left Harvard in 1935 and moved to New York City to be a playwright. Over the years, Eager also wrote lyrics for musicals and adapted operas for television. He would be best known for his children's books, though.

> *"The best kind of magic book . . . is when it's about ordinary people like us, and then something happens and it's magic."*
> —*from* **Seven-Day Magic**

In 1938, Eager married Jane Eberly, whom he had met in high school. They eventually had a son, Fritz. Little Fritz was a redhead, but he was not always happy about his hair color. So in 1951, Eager wrote his first children's book, *Red Head*. Dedicated to Fritz, this book of poems shows how having red hair can be a good thing.

In the early 1950s, the Eagers moved to New Canaan, Connecticut. From their country house by a river, Eager wrote two animal books—*Mouse Manor* and *Playing Possum*.

As he searched for more books to read to his son, Eager discovered the fantasy novels of British author E. Nesbit (Edith Nesbit). He admired

---

EAGER WROTE TWO BOOKS ABOUT ANIMALS BECAUSE HE FELT THAT OTHER ANIMAL BOOKS FOR CHILDREN DID NOT PORTRAY THE CHARACTERS VERY WELL.

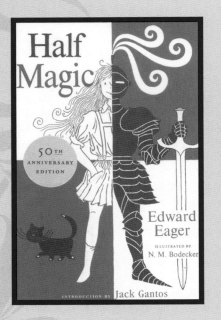

A Selected Bibliography of Eager's Work

Seven-Day Magic (1962)

The Well-Wishers (1960)

Magic or Not? (1959)

The Time Garden (1958)

Magic by the Lake (1957)

Knight's Castle (1956)

Playing Possum (1955)

Half Magic (1954)

Mouse Manor (1952)

Red Head (1951)

them so much that he decided to begin writing the same type of stories. He openly modeled his own fantasies after Nesbit's and even gave her credit in each of his books.

Eager's "daily magic" novels portray ordinary children leading everyday lives until they suddenly discover a magical object. That object transports them into a world of amazing adventures. Eager's first fantasy novel—*Half*

> *"Probably the sincerest compliment I could pay [E. Nesbit] is already paid in the fact that my own books for children could not even have existed if it were not for her influence."*

Magic—was published in 1954. It's a magical tale of four kids who discover a special coin that makes their wishes come only halfway true.

Eager went on to write six more fantasy novels. According to children's author Jack Gantos, Eager's books "have a way of infecting the reader with their charm and cleverness and the belief in the magical, enchanted possibility of everything." Eager died in Stamford, Connecticut, in 1964.

&

WHERE TO FIND OUT MORE ABOUT EDWARD EAGER

BOOKS

Children's Literature Review. Vol. 43. Detroit: Gale, 1997.

Pringle, David, and David Collins, eds. *St. James Guide to Fantasy Writers.* Detroit: St. James Press, 1996.

Silvey, Anita, ed. *The Essential Guide to Children's Books and Their Creators.* Boston: Houghton Mifflin Company, 2002.

Sutherland, Zena. *Children & Books.* 9th ed. Boston: Allyn & Bacon, 1997.

WEB SITES

OXFORD UNIVERSITY PRESS
http://www.oup.co.uk/oxed/children/authors/eager/
To read a short biography of Edward Eager

SF SITE
http://www.sfsite.com/06a/ed58.htm
To read reviews and a biography of Edward Eager

————

EAGER'S HOBBIES INCLUDED BIRD-WATCHING AND GARDENING.

Richard Egielski

Born: July 16, 1952

trange. That is the word that author and illustrator Richard Egielski heard when he first tried to sell his drawings. Some editors thought his drawings were too strange for children's books. Few people think that now. Egielski has illustrated more than thirty children's books and has won many awards.

Richard Egielski was born on July 16, 1952, in New York City. His father was a police lieutenant and his mother was a secretary. His parents called him the artist of the family. Richard began to really study art when he was a

RICHARD EGIELSKI STARTS HIS DRAWINGS WITH A PENCIL. LATER HE GOES BACK OVER THEM WITH WATERCOLOR. HE TRIES TO COMPLETE TWO BOOKS A YEAR.

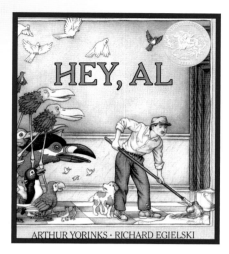

ARTHUR YORINKS · RICHARD EGIELSKI

A Selected Bibliography of Egielski's Work

End (Illustrations only, 2006)
Saint Francis and the Wolf (2005)
Fierce Yellow Pumpkin (Illustrations only, 2003)
Locust Pocus: A Book to Bug You (Illustrations only, 2001)
Three Magic Balls (2000)
The Web Files (Illustrations only, 2000)
One Present from Flekman's (Illustrations only, 1999)
The Tub People's Christmas (Illustrations only, 1999)
Jazper (1998)
The Gingerbread Boy (1997)
Perfect Pancakes, If You Please (Illustrations only, 1997)
Fire! Fire! Said Mrs. McGuire (Illustrations only, 1996)
Buz (1995)
Call Me Ahnighito (Illustrations only, 1995)
The Tub Grandfather (Illustrations only, 1993)
The Lost Sailor (Illustrations only, 1992)
Christmas in July (Illustrations only, 1991)
A Telling of the Tales: Five Stories (Illustrations only, 1990)
Oh, Brother (Illustrations only, 1989)
The Tub People (Illustrations only, 1989)
Friends Forever (Illustrations only, 1988)
Hey, Al (Illustrations only, 1986)
Amy's Eyes (Illustrations only, 1985)
Lower! Higher! You're a Liar! (Illustrations only, 1984)
Getting Even (Illustrations only, 1982)
Mr. Wheatfield's Loft (Illustrations only, 1981)
Finders Weepers (Illustrations only, 1980)
Louis the Fish (Illustrations only, 1980)
I Should Worry, I Should Care (Illustrations only, 1979)
Sid & Sol (Illustrations only, 1977)
The Letter, the Witch, and the Ring (Illustrations only, 1976)
The Porcelain Pagoda (Illustrations only, 1976)

Egielski's Major Literary Award

1987 Caldecott Medal
    Hey, Al

teenager at the High School of Art and Design, a public school in New York City.

Later Egielski studied at the Parsons School of Design. He thought he might become a commercial artist. Then he took a class in picture books taught by Maurice Sendak, the famous children's book author. Sendak inspired Egielski to become an illustrator for children's books.

At the Parsons School of Design, Richard Egielski met

> *"An important teacher is one who exposes you to something new and points out a direction you otherwise might have missed."*

another illustrator—Denise Saldutti. They were married in 1977, three years after Egielski graduated.

Like many authors, Egielski uses experiences from his own life in his books. One time he had Lyme disease. The doctor gave him some medicine to get rid of the bug that was making him sick. Egielski liked the idea of a bug so he used it in the first book that he wrote and illustrated, *Buz.* This story is about a boy who swallows a bug when he is eating his breakfast. The doctor gives the boy some pills to track down the bug in the boy's body. Another of his books, *Jazper,* tells the story of a young boy insect and his father who live in a rented eggshell. The *New York Times* named *Jazper* the best illustrated book of 1998.

Sometimes Richard Egielski works with a partner to make a book. For *Sid & Sol,* Egielski did the illustrations and Arthur Yorinks wrote the text. One of Egielski's former art teachers had told Yorinks about Egielski's drawings and suggested they work together on a project. So they did. Over a period of four-

> *"A good illustrator is never a slave to text. The text rarely tells him what to do, but, rather, what his choices are. I only illustrate texts I truly believe in."*

RICHARD EGIELSKI ENJOYS PLAYING THE MANDOLIN, A STRINGED INSTRUMENT.

teen years, the two men worked on eight books together. One of their books, *Hey, Al,* won the Caldecott Medal in 1987.

Richard Egielski also illustrated a series of books by author Pam Conrad. Conrad wrote stories about the Tub People, a family that lives in a bathroom. Egielski's and Conrad's first book together, *The Tub People,* won the Parents' Choice Picture Book Award in 1989.

"It is through my illustrations that I express myself most deeply and fully," Egielski explains. The illustrator lives in New York City, where he happily continues to create his "strange" drawings.

❧

WHERE TO FIND OUT MORE ABOUT RICHARD EGIELSKI

BOOKS

Cummings, Pat, ed. *Talking with Artists.* 1st ed. New York: Macmillan, 1992.

Holtze, Sally Holmes, ed. *Sixth Book of Junior Authors & Illustrators.*
New York: H. W. Wilson Company, 1989.

Silvey, Anita, ed. *The Essential Guide to Children's Books and Their Creators.*
Boston: Houghton Mifflin, 2002.

WEB SITE

BOOKPEOPLE
http://www.bookpeople.com/infobook.html?isbn=egielskipg
To see samples of Egielski's artwork and
descriptions of his books

———

IN 1997, EGIELSKI WROTE AND ILLUSTRATED
THE GINGERBREAD BOY, BASED ON THE CLASSIC NURSERY RHYME. IN THIS
VERSION, THE GINGERBREAD BOY IS IN NEW YORK, AND RATS, POLICE ON
HORSEBACK, AND CONSTRUCTION WORKERS CHASE HIM!

Lois Ehlert

Born: November 9, 1934

Lois Ehlert creates beautiful picture books for children. Many of them she has written herself. Some of them she has illustrated for other writers. Children and adults have been enjoying her books for thirty years. Ehlert's best-known books include *Color Zoo, Chicka Chicka Boom Boom,* and *Red Leaf, Yellow Leaf.*

Lois Ehlert was born on November 9, 1934, in Beaver Dam, Wisconsin. As a child, Lois enjoyed reading. She, her brother, and her sister used to go to the library each week. Each one checked out five books. During the week, they would trade books and read all fifteen.

Art and creativity was encouraged in Lois's family. Her mother gave her scraps of fabric leftover from sewing projects. Her father gave

———

IN ADDITION TO WRITING AND ILLUSTRATING CHILDREN'S BOOKS, EHLERT HAS ALSO DESIGNED TOYS AND GAMES FOR CHILDREN.

her scraps of wood left over from his projects. "I grew up in a home where everyone seemed to be making something with their hands. As far back as I can remember, I was always putting things together, cutting, stitching, pasting, or pounding. The feel of the object I made was as important as the look," remembers Ehlert.

Lois Ehlert continued creating in high school. She went on to study art at the Layton School of Art in Milwaukee, Wisconsin. After graduating in 1957, she got a job as a graphic designer, illustrating children's books. She wasn't very happy with how the children's books looked when they were published and decided not to do that kind of work anymore.

"As I was growing up, I always wanted to be [an] artist. I didn't know what kind of an artist specifically . . . but I knew that's what I wanted to do."

Several years later, Ehlert decided to try illustrating children's books again. This time, she wrote the story, too. Her first try was *Growing Vegetable Soup.* It was a success! Her next book, *Planting a Rainbow,* was also a success. Ehlert had become a full-time author and illustrator.

Details are important to Ehlert. To get the details right, she does lots of research before starting a book. For *Growing Vegetable Soup,* Ehlert

---

THE CAT IN *FEATHERS FOR LUNCH* WAS BASED ON A REAL CAT.
EHLERT USED HER NEPHEW'S CAT AS THE MODEL.

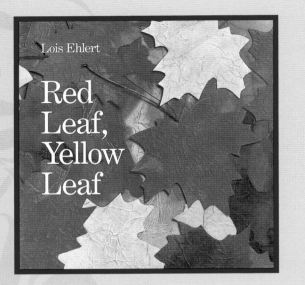

A Selected Bibliography of Ehlert's Work

Leaf Man (2005)

Pie in the Sky (2004)

In My World (2002)

Market Day: A Story Told with Folk Art (2000)

Angel Hide and Seek (Illustrations only, 1998)

Cuckoo: A Mexican Folktale (1997)

Under My Nose (1996)

Snowballs (1995)

Mole's Hill: A Woodland Tale (1994)

Circus (1992)

Red Leaf, Yellow Leaf (1991)

Feathers for Lunch (1990)

Fish Eyes: A Book You Can Count On (1990)

Chicka Chicka Boom Boom (Illustrations only, 1989)

Color Zoo (1989)

Eating the Alphabet: Fruits and Vegetables from A to Z (1989)

Planting a Rainbow (1988)

Growing Vegetable Soup (1987)

Mathematical Games for One or Two (Illustrations only, 1972)

Ehlert's Major Literary Awards

1992 Boston Globe-Horn Book Nonfiction Honor Book
   Red Leaf, Yellow Leaf

1990 Boston Globe-Horn Book Picture Book Honor Book
   Chicka Chicka Boom Boom

1990 Caldecott Honor Book
   Color Zoo

looked at pictures in every seed catalog she could find. For *Fish Eyes: A Book You Can Count On,* Ehlert visited the famous Shedd Aquarium in Chicago. For *Eating the Alphabet: Fruits and Vegetables from A to Z,* Ehlert went to the grocery store every week. She bought the vegetables that were in the book so she had them to look at as she did the illustrations.

Ehlert's ideas come from her everyday experiences. "I

> *"The ideas for my books develop as slowly as seeds I plant in early spring. Ideas and seeds both have to be nurtured to grow. I study, sketch . . . and sit and think."*

realize that I write and draw things I know and care about. Yes, a squirrel really did sneak in through my window. Yes, I do enjoy gardening. Yes, I've made snow creatures, and each year I press beautiful maple leaves in my phone books," says Ehlert.

Ehlert has won many awards for her work. She continues to write and illustrate children's picture books.

WHERE TO FIND OUT MORE ABOUT LOIS EHLERT

BOOKS

McElmeel, Sharron L. *100 Most Popular Picture Book Authors and Illustrators: Biographical Sketches and Bibliographies.* Englewood, Colo.: Libraries Unlimited, 2000.

Silvey, Anita, ed. *The Essential Guide to Children's Books and Their Creators.* Boston: Houghton Mifflin Company, 2002.

WEB SITES

LOIS EHLERT HOME PAGE
http://www.harperchildrens.com/authorintro/index.asp?authorid=12055
To read a biographical sketch of Lois Ehlert

READING IS FUNDAMENTAL
http://www.rif.org/art/illustrators/ehlert.mspx
To read a biographical sketch and find links to other Web resources

EHLERT WEARS OLD CLOTHES AND A DENIM APRON WHEN SHE WORKS.
SHE ADMITS SHE IS MESSY AND DOESN'T CLEAN UP EVERY DAY.

Ed Emberley

Born: October 19, 1931

"I don't really know where I get my ideas. I just tell myself to get an idea and myself does," explains Ed Emberley. Telling himself to get ideas works out very well for Emberley. As the author and illustrator of more than forty books for children, he seems to have plenty of ideas.

Emberley was born in Malden, Massachusetts, on October 19, 1931. One day in first grade, he was drawing a picture of a ship. His

teacher came over and watched him draw. She told him what a nice picture it was. Right then, Ed knew he wanted to be an artist.

In eighth grade, Ed started taking drawing lessons. He found he enjoyed them more than anything else in school. He continued the lessons in high school.

ED EMBERLEY'S FAVORITE PICTURE BOOK IS BEATRIX POTTER'S *THE TALE OF PETER RABBIT.*

Later, he went to the Massachusetts School of Art. There he studied painting and illustration—and met his future wife, Barbara. After college, Emberley served two years in the U.S. Army. Then he went back to school and studied art at the Rhode Island School of Design in Providence.

In 1961, Emberley wrote and illustrated his first book, *The Wing on a Flea: A Book about Shapes.* The book showed children how to see shapes in everyday things. He continued to write and illustrate

"I expect to be one hundred years old when I retire. If I die first, I'll retire then."

A Selected Bibliography of Emberley's Work

Thanks, Mom! (2003)
Ed Emberley's Drawing Book of Trucks and Trains (2002)
Ed Emberley's Drawing Book of Weirdos (2001)
Ed Emberley's Fingerprint Drawing Book (2000)
Three: An Emberley Family Sketchbook (1998)
Glad Monster, Sad Monster: A Book about Feelings (1997)
Go Away, Big Green Monster! (1992)
Animals (1987)
Cars, Boats, and Planes (1987)
Home (1987)
Flash, Crash, Rumble, and Roll (Illustrations only, 1985)
Ed Emberley's ABC (1978)
A Birthday Wish (1977)
The Wizard of Op (1975)
Drawing Books: Make a World (1972)
Clothing (Illustrations only, 1969)
Drummer Hoff (Illustrations only, 1967)
Ladybug, Ladybug, Fly Away Home (Illustrations only, 1967)
One Wide River to Cross (Illustrations only, 1966)
The Wing on a Flea: A Book about Shapes (1961)

Emberley's Major Literary Awards

1968 Caldecott Medal
   Drummer Hoff
1967 Caldecott Honor Book
   One Wide River to Cross

"I started drawing the same time most people do—when I was a little child. Most people stop; I didn't."

children's books, sometimes working with his wife and children. In 1966, Barbara Emberley wrote *One Wide River to Cross,* and Ed illustrated it. Later, Emberley's children, Rebecca and Michael, helped with *Three: An Emberley Family Sketchbook.* Published in 1998, it includes illustrations by Ed Emberley, cutouts by Rebecca Emberley, and comic strip art by Michael Emberley. These days, Emberley's granddaughter helps him with ideas!

Some of Emberley's books use brightly colored woodcuts or clever rhymes to tell a story. Others show young readers how to draw using simple shapes. Some encourage children to come up with new ideas for animals, buildings, and cars. All are illustrated with brilliant colors.

Emberley's drawing books are especially popular. They teach children how to draw everything from grapes to sea monsters. He even has written books showing how to use thumbprints and fingerprints in artwork.

Emberley works on several books at a time and finishes about two books a year. In addition to doing books of his own, he also illustrates books for other people. He has illustrated children's books about computers, science, and the Internet.

EMBERLEY OFTEN ANSWERS HIS READERS' QUESTIONS ABOUT ART VIA E-MAIL. HE EVEN ANSWERS QUESTIONS WHEN HE IS ON VACATION!

His illustrations have won many awards. *One Wide River to Cross* was named a Caldecott Honor Book in 1967. *Drummer Hoff* won a Caldecott Medal in 1968. Barbara Emberley wrote both books.

Ed and Barbara Emberley live in a 300-year-old house in Ipswich, Massachusetts. They enjoy cross-country skiing, sailing, and working on new book ideas together.

WHERE TO FIND OUT MORE ABOUT ED EMBERLEY

BOOKS

Hopkins, Lee Bennett. *Pauses: Autobiographical Reflections of 101 Creators of Children's Books.* New York: HarperCollins, 1995.

Kingman, Lee, Grace Allen Hogarth, and Harriet Quimby, comps. *Illustrators of Children's Books, 1967–1976.* Boston: Horn Book, 1978.

Something about the Author. Vol. 8. Detroit: Gale Research, 1976.

WEB SITES

ED EMBERLEY HOME PAGE
http://www.edemberley.com/pages/main.aspx
For the author's Web site with biographical information, drawings, books, and activities

SCHOLASTIC
http://books.scholastic.com/teachers/authorsandbooks/authorstudies/authorhome.jsp?authorID=33&displayName=Biography
For a biographical sketch of the illustrator and an interview transcript

ED AND BARBARA EMBERLEY OFTEN PRINT CHILDREN'S BOOKS WITH THEIR OWN PRINTING PRESS.

Eleanor Estes

Born: May 9, 1906
Died: July 15, 1988

Eleanor Estes's childhood memories are the basis for the humorous adventures in her books. She is best remembered for the Moffat family and the series that bears their name.

Eleanor Estes was born Eleanor Ruth Rosenfeld in 1906 in West Haven, Connecticut. The third of four children, she grew up with a sister and two brothers. Eleanor's father died when she was thirteen. Her mother then raised the children on her own, working as a dressmaker. She often entertained her children by reciting poetry and telling them folktales.

Eleanor had a happy childhood in Connecticut. In the summer, she and her siblings climbed trees, went fishing, and gathered clams. In the winter, they liked to slide down the snowy hillsides.

THE ESTES'S DAUGHTER, HELENA, WAS BORN IN 1948, AFTER THE COUPLE HAD BEEN MARRIED FOR SIXTEEN YEARS.

> *"I have no aim other than to entertain, and to do this in the most complete and artistic way that I can."*

Eleanor attended elementary school in a one-room schoolhouse. In 1923, she graduated from West Haven High School and went to work in the New Haven Free Public Library as a children's librarian. In 1931, she won a scholarship to study library science at the Pratt Institute in New York City. While she was at Pratt, she met Rice Estes. They married in 1932 and eventually had a daughter, Helena.

Estes began working as a children's librarian at the New York Public Library in 1932. Two years later, she caught tuberculosis. While she recovered, she wrote notes about her childhood memories. She eventually shaped these recollections into many delightful books.

Estes's first book, *The Moffats*, appeared in 1941, and three more Moffat books followed in the years to come. They are set in the fictional town of Cranbury, Connecticut, which Estes modeled after her own hometown of New Haven. Like Estes's family, the Moffat family consists of a widow with four children. The leading character, Janey Moffat, is modeled after Estes herself.

> *"I feel that the impressions I have gathered through the years must be woven into a structure of the imagination—a book written purely for the enjoyment and entertainment of children."*

THE ESTES FAMILY USED TO SPEND THEIR SUMMERS IN EUROPE OR BY THE OCEAN IN ROCKPORT, MASSACHUSETTS.

A Selected Bibliography of Estes's Work

The Curious Adventures of Jimmy McGee (1987)

The Moffat Museum (1983)

The Lost Umbrella of Kim Chu (1978)

The Coat-Hanger Christmas Tree (1973)

The Tunnel of Hugsy Goode (1971)

Miranda the Great (1967)

The Alley (1964)

The Witch Family (1960)

Pinky Pye (1958)

A Little Oven (1955)

Ginger Pye (1951)

The Sleeping Giant and Other Stories (1948)

The Hundred Dresses (1944)

The Sun and the Wind and Mr. Todd (1943)

Rufus M. (1943)

The Middle Moffat (1942)

The Moffats (1941)

Estes's Major Literary Awards

1952 Newbery Medal
Ginger Pye

1945 Newbery Honor Book
The Hundred Dresses

1944 Newbery Honor Book
Rufus M.

1943 Newbery Honor Book
The Middle Moffat

Estes introduced another Cranbury family, the Pyes, in *Ginger Pye* and *Pinky Pye*. In *Ginger Pye*, two children solve the mystery surrounding the disappearance of the family dog, Ginger. *Pinky Pye* features a kitten that can type.

Estes wrote many other books, including mysteries and fantasies. Prejudice is the theme of *The Hundred Dresses*. It's the tale of a Polish girl whose schoolmates ridicule her because she wears only one shabby dress to school. Estes based the story on a girl from her own childhood. She always regretted that she had never reached out in kindness to the girl. She hoped to set things right by writing the book.

In all her stories, Estes captures the childhood years realistically and with warmth, humor, and joy. That is why her books have remained favorites among children for decades. Estes died in Hamden, Connecticut, at the age of eighty-two.

❧

WHERE TO FIND OUT MORE ABOUT ELEANOR ESTES

BOOKS

McElmeel, Sharron L. *100 Most Popular Children's Authors: Biographical Sketches and Bibliographies*. Englewood, Colo.: Libraries Unlimited, 1999.

Silvey, Anita, ed. *The Essential Guide to Children's Books and Their Creators*. Boston: Houghton Mifflin Company, 2002.

Something About the Author. Vol. 91. Detroit: Gale, 1997.

Sutherland, Zena. *Children & Books*. 9th ed. Boston: Allyn & Bacon, 1997.

WEB SITES

EMBRACING THE CHILD
http://www.embracingthechild.org/aestes.html
For a biography of the author

KIDS POINT
http://www.kidspoint.org/columns2.asp?column_id=989&column_type=author
For a profile of the author

———

ESTES DREW HER OWN ILLUSTRATIONS FOR *GINGER PYE* AND SEVERAL OTHER BOOKS.

Ian Falconer

Born: 1959

Imagine what it's like to write and illustrate your first book. You wonder if anyone will read it and like it. Suddenly, you find that everyone *loves* it!

This is what happened to Ian Falconer. He worked for years as an illustrator, stage set designer, and costume designer. Then he wrote and illustrated a children's book. Almost as soon as his book *Olivia* appeared, it became enormously popular. Teachers, parents, and especially children love the humorous book. *Olivia* was named a Caldecott Honor Book in 2001.

THE DRAWINGS OF OLIVIA ARE DONE IN CHARCOAL.

Falconer originally intended the book to be a Christmas present for his niece Olivia. The little girl, clever and lively, had a big imagination and always managed to charm the grown-ups around her. Falconer started working on a book and chose to depict this Olivia as a feisty little pig!

Falconer illustrated Olivia in black and white with splashes of bright red. He even placed an art lesson in the book. When Olivia visits an art gallery, she gazes at a painting of ballet dancers by Edgar Degas. She also looks with confusion at a modern painting by Jackson Pollock.

Falconer's second book for children, *Olivia Saves the Circus,* came out in 2001. In this book, the energetic pig claims she became a great circus performer. She says it happened one day when all the circus people came down with ear infections.

Falconer did not start out to produce books. His first love was art. He was born in Ridgefield, Connecticut, in 1959. After high school, he studied art history at New York University. He also studied painting at the Parsons School of

> *"The real Olivia is an extremely headstrong, imaginative child, who even at the age of three (she is seven now), could argue (or stonewall, or bulldoze, or filibuster) through any 'inconvenience' to achieve her goal."*

IAN FALCONER HAS CREATED THE ARTWORK FOR MORE THAN A DOZEN COVERS OF THE *NEW YORKER* MAGAZINE.

A Selected Bibliography of Falconer's Work

Olivia and the Missing Toy (2003)
Olivia Counts (2002)
Olivia's Opposites (2002)
Olivia Saves the Circus (2001)
Olivia (2000)

Falconer's Major Literary Award

2001 Caldecott Honor Book
  Olivia

Design in New York City and at the Otis Art Institute in Los Angeles, California.

In the 1980s and 1990s, Falconer worked designing stage sets and costumes for operas and ballets. In 1987, he codesigned costumes for the Los Angeles Opera's production of *Tristan und Isolde,* a tragic story of love and death. Later, he created

> *"I intended it originally as a little Christmas present for my niece of the same name. . . . At any rate, the drawings and the character [of Olivia] became better and better, so I began to really develop [the book] in earnest."*

stage sets and costumes for the Chicago Lyric Opera and costumes for the Royal Opera in London.

Ian Falconer has also designed costumes and sets for the New York City Ballet and the Boston Ballet.

Ian Falconer lives in New York City. He enjoys visiting his niece Olivia—and working on his next book about her pig counterpart!

ॐ

WHERE TO FIND OUT MORE ABOUT IAN FALCONER

BOOK

Rockman, Connie C., ed. *The Ninth Book of Junior Authors and Illustrators.* New York: H. W. Wilson Company, 2004.

WEB SITES

KIDSREADS.COM
http://aol.kidsreads.com/authors/au-falconer-ian.asp
To read a brief biographical sketch of Ian Falconer

SIMON & SCHUSTER
http://www.simonsays.com/content/destination.cfm?sid=799&pid=331387&agid=13
For autobiographical information about Ian Falconer

FALCONER HAS DESIGNED FLOATS THAT HAVE APPEARED IN THE MAIN STREET PARADE AT DISNEYLAND IN CALIFORNIA.

Nancy Farmer

Born: July 9, 1941

With an adventurous life of her own, Nancy Farmer was bound to become a great storyteller. Her books for young people range from African tales to science fiction to mythology.

Farmer was born Nancy Forsythe Coe in Phoenix, Arizona, in 1941. She grew up in Yuma, near the Arizona-Mexico border. Her father managed a hotel there, and Nancy began working at the desk when she was nine.

Nancy met plenty of interesting characters at the hotel. Among the regular guests were cowboys, rodeo riders, and circus performers. Sometimes cages full of trained animals crowded the parking lot. One hotel guest was a bank robber, and the police arrested him in his hotel room. Another guest told Nancy about losing his eye in a fight with a grizzly bear.

FARMER'S GRANDFATHER DIDN'T LIKE TRICK-OR-TREATERS. ON HALLOWEEN, HE WOULD SIT ON THE FRONT PORCH WITH A SHOTGUN TO SCARE THEM OFF.

Nancy wasn't very interested in school, and she sometimes played hooky. Nevertheless, she managed to earn a degree from Reed College in Portland, Oregon, in 1963. Searching for adventure, she traveled to India to work in the Peace Corps (a volunteer organization that works to improve conditions in foreign countries) from 1963 to 1965.

In 1971, she went to Africa, where she spent the next seventeen years. For much of that time, she worked with scientists studying insects and water purity in Mozambique and Zimbabwe. Her work took her to many remote villages, and she often encountered wild animals. In 1976, she met Harold Farmer,

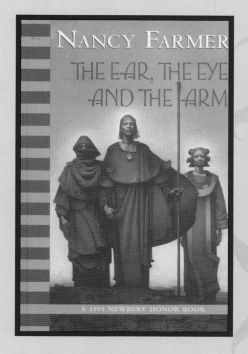

A Selected Bibliography of Farmer's Work

The Sea of Trolls (2004)
The House of the Scorpion (2002)
Casey Jones's Fireman (1998)
A Girl Named Disaster (1996)
Runnery Granary (1996)
The Warm Place (1995)
Do You Know Me? (1993)
Tapiwa's Uncle (1993)
The Ear, the Eye, and the Arm (1989)
Tsitsi's Skirt (1988)
Lorelei: The Story of a Bad Cat (1987)

Farmer's Major Literary Awards

2003 Newbery Honor Book
2002 National Book Award
  The House of the Scorpion

1997 Newbery Honor Book
  A Girl Named Disaster

1995 Newbery Honor Book
  The Ear, the Eye, and the Arm

> *"My first aim is to entertain, to keep young readers riveted. Secondly, I want them to come away with the feeling that they can be strong, that they can do things—and that they mustn't give in."*

an English professor at the University of Zimbabwe in Rukomeche. They married six months later. They continued living in Zimbabwe, where they had a son, Daniel.

Farmer stayed home to care for Daniel, and she read books to keep busy. One day while reading, she thought, "I can do this!" She sat down and wrote a short story, and she just kept writing. Her first book, *Lorelei: The Story of a Bad Cat*, was published in Zimbabwe in 1987.

Farmer wrote several more books in Zimbabwe. Most are centered on African themes and portray tribal life and traditions. Her science fiction novel *The Ear, the Eye, and the Arm* tells the story of three Zimbabwean children in the year 2194.

The Farmers decided to return to the United States in 1988. Zimbabwe was wracked with disease and political unrest, and they didn't think it was a safe place for Daniel. The family settled in California, and Harold began teaching at the University of California at Berkeley.

Meanwhile, Farmer kept writing. Her novel *Do You Know Me?* is the story of a girl who lives in Zimbabwe, while *The Warm Place* tells

IN MOZAMBIQUE, FARMER LIVED BY LAKE CABORA BASSA. THIS AREA BECAME THE SETTING FOR HER BOOK *A GIRL NAMED DISASTER*.

about a baby giraffe that escapes from a zoo and returns to Africa. *A Girl Named Disaster* recounts an African girl's terrifying journey to escape an arranged marriage. In *The House of the Scorpion*, Farmer tackles the issue of human cloning. *The Sea of Trolls* deals with the Vikings of Norse mythology.

Farmer continues to write books from her home in Menlo Park, California.

> *"The character, viewpoint, and zany sense of humor of the people I met [in Africa] have had a major effect on my writing."*

∞

WHERE TO FIND OUT MORE ABOUT NANCY FARMER

BOOKS

Pendergast, Tom, and Sara Pendergast, eds. *St. James Guide to Young Adult Writers.* 2nd ed. Detroit: St. James Press, 1999.

Silvey, Anita, ed. *The Essential Guide to Children's Books and Their Creators.* Boston: Houghton Mifflin Company, 2002.

WEB SITES

FIRST PERSON BOOK PAGE
http://www.bookpage.com/0410bp/nancy_farmer.html
To read an interview with the author

TEENS POINT
http://www.teenspoint.org/reading_matters/columns2.asp?column_id=1153&column_type=tpauthprofile
For an author profile of Nancy Farmer

———

FROM 1969 TO 1971, FARMER STUDIED CHEMISTRY AT MERRITT COLLEGE IN OAKLAND, CALIFORNIA, AND THE UNIVERSITY OF CALIFORNIA AT BERKELEY.

Anne Fine

Born: December 7, 1947

Anne Fine has a gift for communicating with readers of all ages. She is the author of more than forty books, ranging from children's picture books to young-adult fiction to adult novels.

Anne Fine was born Anne Laker in Leicester, England. She grew up in the country with her four sisters, three of whom were triplets. Anne learned to read when she was very young, and she loved it.

"When I was a child, I read all the time," she recalls. "On buses. In the garden. In bed. Under the table at mealtimes." Although she never thought of becoming a writer, she had lots of practice. Every Monday morning, her teacher at primary school made the students write a story.

IN 2003, FINE WAS NAMED OFFICER OF THE BRITISH EMPIRE (OBE) FOR HER SERVICE TO CHILDREN'S LITERATURE. GREAT BRITAIN GRANTS THIS TITLE TO CITIZENS WHO HAVE GIVEN EXCEPTIONAL SERVICE IN THEIR FIELD.

Anne attended Northampton High School for Girls in Northampton, England. The teachers were strict, but Anne enjoyed the quiet, orderly atmosphere. Then in 1965, she began classes at the University of Warwick in Coventry, England. She majored in history and politics. In 1968, while still at the university, she met a philosopher named Kit Fine, and they married six weeks later. The couple eventually had two daughters.

After graduation in 1968, Fine taught English for a year at Cardinal Wiseman Secondary School, a girls' school in Coventry. In 1969, the Fines moved to Oxford, England. There she worked for two years for the Oxford Committee for Famine Relief (OXFAM).

One day in 1971, a snowstorm kept Fine from going out. Trapped in her chilly apartment, she began writing to cheer herself up. This resulted in her first novel, *The Summer-House Loon*, which was published in 1978 (1979 in the United States). It was followed by a steady stream of books.

Meanwhile, because of her husband's job, the family moved around a lot, living in Scotland, Canada, and the United States. The couple eventually divorced,

> *"I still work in pencil. . . . I'll write a whole chapter this way, writing, erasing, writing again, over and over until I'm sure it's right. Then I'll type it up, and start to alter it again."*

FINE WORKED AS A TEACHER AT SAUGHTON JAIL IN EDINBURGH, SCOTLAND, FROM 1971 TO 1972. SHE CLAIMS IT WAS NOT AS TIRING AS HER JOB TEACHING AT A GIRLS' SCHOOL.

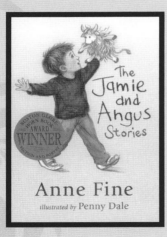

A Selected Bibliography of Fine's Work

Countdown (2006)
Frozen Billy (2006)
Notso Hotso (2006)
The Jamie and Angus Stories (2002)
Bad Dreams (2000)
The Tulip Touch (1997)
Flour Babies (1994)
Goggle-Eyes (1989)
Alias Madame Doubtfire (1988)
The Granny Project (1983)
The Summer-House Loon (1979)

Fine's Major Literary Awards

2003 Boston Globe–Horn Book Fiction Award
   The Jamie and Angus Stories

1994 Boston Globe–Horn Book Fiction Honor Book
1992 Carnegie Medal
   Flour Babies

1989 Carnegie Medal
   Goggle-Eyes

and Anne and the girls settled in Edinburgh, Scotland, in 1981. She later married Richard Warren, a scientist and father of two.

Many of Fine's novels are about teenagers and the problems they face growing up. Some are lighthearted and full of comic situations. Others deal with serious themes such as divorce, homelessness, and crime. For example, *Goggle-Eyes* was

"Never show your [writing] work to a family member. . . . Even if they say it is very good, there is still something about the way they say it that makes you want to kill them."

made into a prime-time British TV series. Another novel, *Alias Madame Doubtfire*, was the basis for the 1993 movie *Mrs. Doubtfire*, starring Robin Williams.

Fine was chosen as Great Britain's Children's Laureate for 2001 to 2003. This honor is given to a children's book author or illustrator who is outstanding in his or her field. As a laureate, Fine traveled around the country promoting literacy, libraries, and children's literature.

Fine and her husband currently live in a stone house by a river in the little town of Barnard Castle in County Durham, England.

⚬

WHERE TO FIND OUT MORE ABOUT ANNE FINE

BOOKS

Authors and Artists for Young Adults. Vol. 20. Detroit: Gale, 1997.

Pendergast, Sara, and Tom Pendergast, eds. *St. James Guide to Children's Writers*. 5th ed. Detroit: St. James Press, 1999.

Silvey, Anita, ed. *The Essential Guide to Children's Books and Their Creators*. Boston: Houghton Mifflin Company, 2002.

WEB SITES

ANNE FINE
http://www.annefine.co.uk/
For a biography, news, FAQs, and awards

WALKER BOOKS
http://www.walkerbooks.co.uk/Anne-Fine
For a biography and a list of things to know about Anne Fine

FINE DISLIKES SHOPPING, AND SHE SAYS SHE WEARS HER CLOTHES UNTIL THEY ARE COMPLETELY WORN OUT.

Louise Fitzhugh

Born: October 5, 1928
Died: November 19, 1974

Louise Fitzhugh was not afraid to write about controversial subjects. Many people love her frank novels for young readers. But others have banned her book *Harriet the Spy* from some school libraries. They say the idea of spying encourages children to be dishonest and secretive. In *Harriet the Spy,* eleven-year-old Harriet writes about her classmates and neighbors in a secret notebook and then must suffer the consequences when she loses it.

Louise Fitzhugh was born on October 5, 1928, in Memphis, Tennessee. Even though her family was wealthy, Louise did not have a happy childhood. Shortly after Louise was born, her parents were divorced. Both Louise's mother and father wanted custody of their daughter. After a long struggle in

---

HARRIET THE SPY WAS ADAPTED AS A MOTION PICTURE AND RELEASED IN **1996**.

a court, her father, a wealthy attorney, received full custody of Louise. She grew up without ever knowing her mother. This caused feelings of loneliness that she later drew on for her books.

Louise enjoyed reading as a young child. She began writing her own stories when she was about eleven years old.

When she finished high school, Louise Fitzhugh wanted to leave the South. She was troubled by the racism and bigotry in Memphis and did not agree with how many people treated African Americans in the South. She studied literature at three different colleges in Florida and New York. Her interest turned to art, and she left college before earning her degree.

A Selected Bibliography of Fitzhugh's Work

I Am Four (Text only, 1982)
Sport (1979)
I Am Five (1978)
Nobody's Family Is Going to Change (1974)
The Long Secret (1965)
Harriet the Spy (1964)
Suzuki Beane (Illustrations only, 1961)

> *"Ole Golly says there is as many ways to live as there are people on the earth and I shouldn't go round with blinders but should see every way I can. Then I'll know what way I want to live and not just live like my family."*
>
> —*from* **Harriet the Spy**

Then Fitzhugh studied at two art schools in New York City. She also went to Europe to study art. After returning to New York City, she became a well-respected artist. Many of her oil paintings were exhibited in galleries around the country.

Fitzhugh also continued to write. Much of her writing was in the form of unpublished novels and plays for adults. Her first published children's book was *Suzuki Beane,* which she illustrated for her friend and author Sandra Scoppettone.

Fitzhugh continued work on her own book about the independent young Harriet. She had trouble finding a company to publish the novel. Finally, in 1964, *Harriet the Spy* was published.

> *"Cook settled herself with a cup of coffee. 'How long you been a spy?' Since I could write. Ole Golly told me if I was going to be a writer I better write down everything, so I'm a spy that writes down everything."*
>
> —*from* **Harriet the Spy**

FITZHUGH'S BOOK *NOBODY'S FAMILY IS GOING TO CHANGE* WAS USED AS THE BASIS FOR THE BROADWAY MUSICAL *THE TAP DANCE KID.*

Fitzhugh's career as a children's author lasted only thirteen years. Louise Fitzhugh died of a burst blood vessel on November 19, 1974, at the age of forty-six. Her third novel, *Nobody's Family Is Going to Change,* was published one week after her death.

◆

WHERE TO FIND OUT MORE ABOUT LOUISE FITZHUGH

BOOKS

Collier, Laurie, and Joyce Nakamura, eds. *Authors & Artists for Young Adults.* Vol. 18. Detroit: Gale Research, 1996.

Marcus, Leonard S., ed. *Dear Genius: The Letters of Ursula Nordstrom.* New York: HarperCollins, 1998.

McElmeel, Sharron L. *100 Most Popular Children's Authors: Biographical Sketches and Bibliographies.* Englewood, Colo.: Libraries Unlimited, 1999.

Silvey, Anita, ed. *The Essential Guide to Children's Books and Their Creators.* Boston: Houghton Mifflin Company, 2002.

Wolf, Virginia L. *Louise Fitzhugh.* New York: Twayne Publishers, 1991.

WEB SITE
SIMON & SCHUSTER
http://www.simonsays.com/content/destination.cfm?sid=799&pid=331387&agid=13
To read about the author

HARRIET THE SPY HAS SOLD MORE THAN 2.5 MILLION COPIES SINCE IT WAS PUBLISHED IN 1964.

Sharon G. Flake

Born: December 24, 1955

haron G. Flake novels are realistic and sometimes harsh, but they're always full of hope. They explore the lives of African American preteens and teenagers. Flake draws on her own background to portray her characters and their struggles in inner-city neighborhoods.

Sharon Geraldine Flake was born in Philadelphia, Pennsylvania, in 1955. She grew up on the rough streets of North Philadelphia.

Fortunately, Sharon and her five siblings enjoyed the security and support of loving parents and a close-knit family.

Sharon was not good at grammar and spelling in school, so she never thought of becoming a writer. Her self-esteem was not high, either. "[W]hen I was in middle school," she recalls, "I felt very small and insecure. . . . I didn't think I was pretty or

FLAKE ENJOYS GARDENING AND COLLECTING AFRICAN AMERICAN DOLLS.

> *"[This] is America; every-one can be published once. But if you want to be published more than once, and have a career in writing, you need to learn to do it well."*

smart enough. I would stay in my house a lot and read books and watch TV rather than going out."

Flake enrolled in the University of Pittsburgh, hoping to become a doctor. But she kept changing majors and finally decided to study English. It wasn't long before she began writing stories for her classes. Although her teachers told her she was talented, Flake had trouble accepting their encouragement. She figured they were just being nice.

After earning her degree in 1978, Flake decided to work at the University of Pittsburgh, where she held various jobs in communications and public relations. Flake's day jobs gave her plenty of opportunities to sharpen her writing skills. She also worked on articles for national publications, including *Essence* and *Black Elegance* magazines. She started sending her fiction stories to publishers, too, even though she received many rejections at first.

> *"I think there are not nearly enough black writers who do young-adult books. Our kids go to bookstores, and they don't find anything."*

FROM ABOUT 1976 TO 1983, FLAKE WORKED AS A YOUTH COUNSELOR FOR THE CENTER FOR THE ASSESSMENT AND TREATMENT OF YOUTH, A FOSTER CARE AGENCY IN PITTSBURGH.

A Selected Bibliography of Flake's Work

Bang! (2005)

Who Am I without Him? Short Stories about Boys and the Girls in Their Lives (2004)

Begging for Change (2003)

Money Hungry (2001)

The Skin I'm In (1998)

Flake didn't have much time to dwell on these rejections—she was busy raising her daughter, Brittney. When Brittney was young, Flake began writing what eventually became her first published book. It took two years to finish, but *The Skin I'm In* finally appeared in 1998. It's the story of an African American girl who learns to love who she is.

The Skin I'm In was a great success with young readers. African American kids especially liked having characters who spoke the way they did and faced the same struggles. At last, Flake understood that she had a talent for writing and continued to work at it.

Flake's next book, *Money Hungry*, is about an inner-city

teenage girl who will do just about anything to make money. The girl's story continues in *Begging for Change*, as she struggles to escape the cycle of poverty. *Who Am I without Him? Short Stories about Boys and the Girls in Their Lives* is a collection of short stories about African American girls and their issues with the boys in their lives. The gritty novel *Bang!* follows the struggles of an inner-city boy whose brother has been shot. With each new book, Flake gains more enthusiastic readers.

Today, Flake still lives and works in Pittsburgh. She enjoys visiting urban schools and libraries and talking to kids about their lives and dreams.

❧

WHERE TO FIND OUT MORE ABOUT
SHARON G. FLAKE

BOOK
Rockman, Connie C., ed. *The Ninth Book of Junior Authors and Illustrators.*
New York: H. W. Wilson Company, 2004.

WEB SITES
LIVE WORLD
http://www.liveworld.com/transcripts/NYPL/7-18-2002.1-1.html
To read an interview with Sharon G. Flake

SHARON G. FLAKE
http://www.sharongflake.com/
To read a brief biography of the author

FLAKE'S FAVORITE SPORT IS TRACK, AND HER FAVORITE FOOD IS CHOCOLATE.

Paul Fleischman

Born: September 5, 1952

lthough he is the author of more than twenty books, Paul Fleischman never dreamed he would turn out to be a writer. As a child, he wasn't even much of a reader.

Paul Fleischman was born on September 5, 1952, in Monterey, California, and grew up in Santa Monica. He preferred riding his bike and hanging out on the beach to reading.

Paul's father was a writer, however. Sid Fleischman, who won the Newbery Medal in 1987 for *The Whipping Boy,* often read his unfinished book chapters to his family. Sometimes he asked his wife and children what they thought should happen next. Young Paul loved suggesting ideas to his dad.

———

WHEN PAUL FLEISCHMAN WAS GROWING UP, THE FAMILY SELDOM WATCHED TELEVISION. THEY PREFERRED READING AND PLAYING MUSIC TOGETHER.

Music was a part of everyday life in the Fleischman home. Paul and his mother played piano, and his father played the guitar. Later in life, Paul Fleischman learned to play the recorder. He also played the accordion and wrote music.

Today, Fleischman is a well-known author of historical novels and poems. Novels give him a chance to do all kinds of historical research. He compares his research to a detective game in which he tracks down unusual bits of information. Fleischman makes sure that his books accurately depict the clothing, language, environment, and ideas of the times in which they are set.

> *"I never dreamed of becoming a writer. I didn't know what I wanted to be as a child—or a young adult."*

Many of his books take place in the eighteenth and nineteenth centuries. They include people from all walks of life—from servants to military leaders to Native Americans. Some of his books tell the story from several different points of view. In *Bull Run,* sixteen people tell their own versions of a Civil War battle. *Saturnalia* is set in 1681 in Boston, Massachusetts. It describes masters, servants, tradesmen, and apprentices.

Fleischman's poetry also has many voices. His books of poetry include *I Am Phoenix: Poems for Two Voices; Joyful Noise: Poems for Two*

THE FLEISCHMAN FAMILY HAD AN OLD-FASHIONED PRINTING PRESS. PAUL AND HIS SISTERS USED IT TO MAKE STATIONERY AND BUSINESS CARDS.

A Selected Bibliography of Fleischman's Work

Zap (2005)
Sidewalk Circus (2004)
The Animal Hedge (2003)
Seek (2001)
Big Talk: Poems for Four Voices (2000)
Whirligig (1998)
Seedfolks (1997)
Dateline: Troy (1996)
The Borning Room (1993)
Bull Run (1993)
Saturnalia (1990)
Joyful Noise: Poems for Two Voices (1988)
Coming-and-Going Men: Four Tales (1985)
I Am Phoenix: Poems for Two Voices (1985)
Graven Images: Three Stories (1982)

Fleischman's Major Literary Awards

1994 Scott O'Dell Award
   Bull Run

1990 Boston Globe–Horn Book Fiction Honor Book
   Saturnalia

1989 Newbery Medal
1988 Boston Globe–Horn Book Fiction Honor Book
   Joyful Noise: Poems for Two Voices

1983 Newbery Honor Book
   Graven Images: Three Stories

Voices; and *Big Talk: Poems for Four Voices.* The poems in these collections are meant to be read aloud by several people. Some lines are read by one person alone, and some are read by everyone together, like a choir with solos and harmony singing. It is easy to see that Fleischman's musical background has influenced his writing.

In *Seek,* Fleischman builds on the idea of having many voices. *Seek* is the story of Rob, who is looking for the father he

> *"I do lots of research for my historical novels. It takes many fat books in order to write one thin one."*

never knew. Altogether, fifty-two different people enter Rob's story. The story is meant to be read aloud like a play.

Paul Fleischman is married and has two children. He lives in Monterey, California.

WHERE TO FIND OUT MORE ABOUT PAUL FLEISCHMAN

BOOKS

McElmeel, Sharron L. *100 Most Popular Children's Authors : Biographical Sketches and Bibliographies.* Englewood, Colo.: Libraries Unlimited, 1999.

Pendergast, Tom, and Sara Pendergast, eds.
St. James Guide to Young Adult Writers. 2nd ed.
Detroit: St. James Press, 1999.

Silvey, Anita, ed. *The Essential Guide to Children's Books and Their Creators.*
Boston: Houghton Mifflin, 2002.

WEB SITES

PAUL FLEISCHMAN HOME PAGE
http://www.paulfleischman.net/
To read a brief biographical sketch of Paul Fleischman and detailed information about his books

TEENREADS.COM
http://www.teenreads.com/authors/au-fleischman-paul.asp
To read an interview with Paul Fleischman

IN RECENT YEARS, FLEISCHMAN HAS WRITTEN SCREENPLAYS FOR TWO
OF HIS BOOKS. HE HAS ALSO WRITTEN A PLAY CALLED *ZAP.*

Sid Fleischman

Born: March 16, 1920

Before he became a Newbery Medal–winning author, Sid Fleischman entertained people as a professional magician! He traveled around the country entertaining people with his magic. Though his days as a magician are behind him, he still entertains people—with his books. Fleischman has written novels and screenplays for adults. He is best known as the author of the Josh McBroom series, the Bloodhound Gang series, and *The Whipping Boy,* a story about the adventures of a royal prince and an orphan boy who receives a whipping whenever the young prince does something wrong.

Albert Sidney Fleischman was born on March 16, 1920, in Brooklyn, New York. He grew up in San Diego, California. As a

IN 1987, FLEISCHMAN WON THE NEWBERY MEDAL FOR *THE WHIPPING BOY.* TWO YEARS LATER, HIS SON, PAUL FLEISCHMAN, WON THE SAME AWARD FOR HIS BOOK, *JOYFUL NOISE: POEMS FOR TWO VOICES.*

young boy, Sid was interested in storytelling, but he did not think about being a writer. He wanted to be a magician, so he read as many books as he could about magic tricks. Sid practiced tricks and even invented some tricks of his own.

Sid Fleischman decided to write a book that included some of his magic tricks. *Between Cocktails* was published when he

"*I suspect my magician's mind reveals itself in the way I plot my scenes and write my characters. I cannot resist mystery, surprise, and heroes capable of a kind of sleight-of-mind in outwitting the villains.*"

A Selected Bibliography of Fleischman's Work

Escape! The Story of the Great Houdini (2006)
Disappearing Act (2003)
Bo & Mzzz Mad (2001)
A Carnival of Animals (2000)
McBroom Tells a Lie (1999)
Bandit's Moon (1998)
Chancy and the Grand Rascal (1997)
The Abracadabra Kid: A Writer's Life (1996)
13th Floor: A Ghost Story (1995)
Here Comes McBroom: Three More Tall Tales (1992)
The Midnight Horse (1990)
The Scarebird (1988)
The Whipping Boy (1986)
McBroom Tells the Truth (1981)
Humbug Mountain (1978)
McBroom and the Beanstalk (1978)
Jingo Django (1971)
Longbeard the Wizard (1970)
The Ghost in the Noonday Sun (1965)
By the Great Horn Spoon! (1963)
Mr. Mysterious & Company (1962)

Fleischman's Major Literary Awards

1987 Newbery Medal
The Whipping Boy

1979 Boston Globe–Horn Book Fiction Award
Humbug Mountain

was just seventeen years old! "When I saw my name on the cover, I was hooked on writing books," Fleischman says.

After he finished high school, Sid Fleischman traveled around the country entertaining people with his magic act. He heard many stories and folktales from people he met in small towns. Many of these stories later influenced his writing. He served in the U.S. Naval Reserve during World War II (1939–1945). When he left the military in 1945, he took a job at a newspaper in San Diego.

> *"The books we enjoy as children stay with us forever—they have a special impact. Paragraph after paragraph, and page after page, the author must deliver his or her best work."*

In 1951, Fleischman began his career as a full-time writer. He started out writing for adults. His own children did not understand what he did for a living. "I decided to clear up the mystery and wrote a book just for them," Fleischman explains. He wanted his children to know that he earned money by writing. The story that Fleischman wrote for his children became *Mr. Mysterious & Company*. His first children's book, it was published in 1962.

An important part of Fleischman's writing for children is humor. He is also known for using crazy names for characters in his books.

IT TOOK FLEISCHMAN ALMOST TEN YEARS TO WRITE *THE WHIPPING BOY*. HE THOUGHT OF THE IDEA FOR THE BOOK WHILE DOING RESEARCH FOR ANOTHER BOOK.

"I collect interesting names, funny names, and outrageous names, and sometimes the name itself helps me to create a character," he explains.

Fleischman lives near the Pacific Ocean in Santa Monica, California. He has written more than fifty books for young people and adults.

❧

WHERE TO FIND OUT MORE ABOUT SID FLEISCHMAN

BOOKS

Cart, Michael. *What's So Funny: Wit and Humor in American Children's Literature.* New York: HarperCollins, 1995.

Fleischman, Sid. *The Abracadabra Kid: A Writer's Life.* New York: Greenwillow Books, 1996.

McElmeel, Sharron L. *100 Most Popular Children's Authors: Biographical Sketches and Bibliographies.* Englewood, Colo.: Libraries Unlimited, 1999.

Rockman, Connie C., ed. *The Ninth Book of Junior Authors and Illustrators.* New York: H. W. Wilson Company, 2004.

Silvey, Anita, ed. *The Essential Guide to Children's Books and Their Creators.* Boston: Houghton Mifflin Company, 2002.

WEB SITES

RANDOM HOUSE: SID FLEISCHMAN

http://www.randomhouse.com/author/results.pperl?authorid=8841
To find out about Sid Fleischman's favorite books, hobbies, and foods

SID FLEISCHMAN HOME PAGE

http://www.sidfleischman.com/
To read more about Sid Fleischman's life, to find answers to questions for his readers, and to read some of his tips for young writers

———

FLEISCHMAN'S *BY THE GREAT HORN SPOON!* WAS ADAPTED INTO THE 1967 MOVIE CALLED *THE ADVENTURES OF BULLWHIP GRIFFIN*. HIS BOOK *THE GHOST IN THE NOONDAY SUN* WAS ALSO MADE INTO A MOVIE, WHICH WAS RELEASED IN 1974.

Denise Fleming

Born: January 31, 1950

Most people imagine an artist as someone working with pencils or paintbrushes. But Denise Fleming is different. She starts her art projects with tubs of soft, colored mush. Fleming uses the mush to make her own paper. When she's finished, she has thick, wet sheets with the images set right in.

Denise Fleming was born on January 31, 1950, in Toledo, Ohio. As a child, she and her younger sister liked to spend their free time outdoors. They rode bikes, ran races, and put on plays for their friends. In school, Denise especially liked art classes. When she was only a third-grader, she was chosen to take art classes at the local art museum. One of

FLEMING'S HUSBAND, DAVID, AND DAUGHTER, INDIGO, HELP IN THE PAPERMAKING PROCESS. DAVID MAKES THE STENCILS, AND ALL THREE DISCUSS PICTURE IDEAS FOR BOOKS.

her paintings received a special honor. It was picked to be on the cover of a teachers' magazine!

Denise Fleming's parents were also creative. Her father had a workshop in the basement where he built furniture. Her mother was active in the local theater. Both parents encouraged Denise's creativity and artwork. Denise loved to spend hours in the basement while her dad worked on furniture. She would find her own space and make things out of papier-mâché and wood.

> *"The whole process [of papermaking] is wet, messy, and wonderful."*

In high school, Denise took art classes and won several art awards. Then she moved to Michigan and went to Kendall College of Art and Design. In college, she met another artist named David Powers. Powers and Fleming got married after college and went to work.

For a while, Fleming illustrated children's books written by other people. In time, she decided she would rather work on her own projects. She quit her job, and she and her husband delved into different kinds of art, carpentry, and furniture building.

Then Fleming and her sister took a class in papermaking. They learned about making pulp and how to turn it into paper. Fleming loved the class and took another one. Soon she began experimenting on her own. She enjoyed sinking her hands into the thick, wet pulp,

———

DENISE FLEMING TOOK AN ART CLASS AT A MUSEUM IN THE THIRD GRADE. SOME OF HER PICTURES WERE PICKED TO BE IN AN ART EXCHANGE PROGRAM WITH OTHER COUNTRIES.

In the
Small, Small Pond

Denise Fleming

A Selected Bibliography of Fleming's Work

Cow Who Clucked (2006)
First Day of Winter (2005)
Buster (2003)
Alphabet under Construction (2002)
Pumpkin Eye (2001)
The Everything Book (2000)
Mama Cat Has Three Kittens (1998)
Time to Sleep (1997)
Where Once There Was a Wood (1996)
Barnyard Banter (1994)
In the Small, Small Pond (1993)
Count! (1992)
Lunch (1992)
In the Tall, Tall Grass (1991)

Fleming's Major Literary Awards

1994 Caldecott Honor Book
  In the Small, Small Pond

1992 Boston Globe–Horn Book Picture Book Award
  In the Tall, Tall Grass

mixing colors into it, and seeing how the colors and fibers blended.

Fleming developed a way of making pictures by pushing colored pulp through stencils. The result is a rich, colorful image built right into the paper. Sometimes the pulp seems to have a mind of its own. In the finished artwork, some areas of color have sharp, clear edges. Other areas have soft edges where colors have seeped into each other. Some colors are strong and solid. Others are mottled or speckled.

Fleming calls her works "pulp paintings." She used them to illustrate her 1991 book for small children, *In the Tall, Tall, Grass*. The book is full of short rhymes and colorful close-ups of animals. In 1993, she wrote *In the Small, Small Pond* and again used pulp paintings. This book was named a Caldecott Honor Book for its splendid illustrations.

> *"I haven't picked up a brush or a colored pencil since I discovered papermaking."*

Today, Denise Fleming continues to write and illustrate books for young children. She lives in Toledo, Ohio, with her husband, their daughter, Indigo, and many, many cats.

&

WHERE TO FIND OUT MORE ABOUT DENISE FLEMING

BOOKS

McElmeel, Sharron L. *Children's Authors and Illustrators Too Good to Miss: Biographical Sketches and Bibliographies*. Englewood, Colo: Libraries Unlimited, 2004.

Something about the Author. Vol. 126. Detroit: Gale Research, 2002.

WEB SITES

DENISE FLEMING HOME PAGE
http://denisefleming.com/
To visit Fleming's Web site and download her papermaking and bookbinding instructions

KIDSREADS.COM
http://www.kidsreads.com/authors/au-fleming-denise.asp
To read a short biography of Fleming and some fun facts about her

FLEMING'S BOOK *MAMA CAT HAS THREE KITTENS* IS DEDICATED TO ABIGAIL, THE FIRST CAT SHE HAD AS A CHILD.

Esther Forbes

Born: June 28, 1891
Died: August 12, 1967

A passion for history ran in Esther Forbes's family. Forbes's mother had an attic full of old books about New England history. As a child, Esther Forbes loved to page through the history books. In fact, the Forbes family was itself a part of New England history. In the 1600s, one of Esther Forbes's ancestors was accused of

being a witch. She died in jail.

Esther Forbes used her passion for New England history to write biographies and historical novels. She was born on June 28, 1891, in Westborough, Massachusetts. Her father, William Trowbridge Forbes, was a judge. Her mother, Harriet Merrifield Forbes, was a writer and local historian. Forbes attended

DURING WORLD WAR I (1914–1918), ESTHER FORBES LEFT COLLEGE TO WORK ON A FARM IN WEST VIRGINIA. THE CROPS GROWN THERE SUPPORTED THE U.S. WAR EFFORT.

Bradford Academy and the University of Wisconsin.

In 1920, Forbes began working as an editor at the Houghton Mifflin publishing company. She also began working on her own writing. In 1926, she published her first

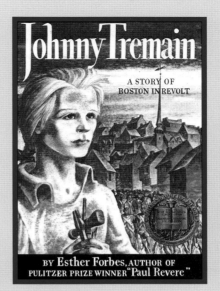

> *"Already on every village green throughout New England, men and boys were drilling in defiance of the King's orders. They said they were afraid of an attack from the French. These men had no uniforms. They came from the fields and farms in the very clothes they used for plowing."—from* **Johnny Tremain**

A Selected Bibliography of Forbes's Work
America's Paul Revere (1946)
Johnny Tremain (1943)

Forbes's Major Literary Award
1944 Newbery Medal
  Johnny Tremain

> "His hand came down on top of the furnace. The burn was so terrible he at first felt no pain, but stood stupidly looking at his hand. For one second, before the metal cooled, the inside of his right hand, from wrist to fingertips, was coated with solid silver."
>
> —*from* **Johnny Tremain**

novel for adult readers, called *O Genteel Lady!* She published five more novels in the next twelve years. One of them, *A Mirror for Witches,* was based on the story of her ancestor who had been charged with witchcraft.

In 1943, Esther Forbes published a biography of the patriot Paul Revere. *Paul Revere and the World He Lived In* describes Revere's life as well as everyday life in Boston in the 1700s. Forbes's mother helped her research the book, which won the 1943 Pulitzer Prize for history.

Forbes and her mother gathered so much interesting research that Forbes decided to write another book. *Johnny Tremain* is set in Boston at the beginning of the American Revolution. The title character is a silver-smith's apprentice. (A silversmith makes objects of silver. An apprentice is a worker learning a trade from a master craftsman.) *Johnny Tremain,* the only novel Forbes wrote for young readers, became her best-known work.

In the book, Johnny Tremain becomes involved with a group of patriots fighting against the British after an accident prevents him from

ESTHER FORBES ONCE SAID THAT SHE HOPED *JOHNNY TREMAIN* WOULD "SHOW THE BOYS AND GIRLS OF TODAY HOW DIFFICULT WERE THOSE OTHER CHILDREN'S LIVES BY MODERN STANDARDS."

becoming a silversmith. The story puts Tremain in the midst of many real historic events, including the Boston Tea Party. As a messenger for the American patriots, Tremain meets John Hancock, Samuel Adams, and other patriots. Paul Revere also appears as a character in the book. In the process of helping win American independence from Britain, Tremain begins to grow to manhood.

Like *Paul Revere and the World He Lived In, Johnny Tremain* won high praise from critics and readers. The book won the 1944 Newbery Medal. *Johnny Tremain* is today considered a classic of children's literature. In 1946, Esther Forbes wrote another book about Paul Revere. Called *America's Paul Revere,* this biography was also for young readers. Esther Forbes died on August 12, 1967, at the age of seventy-six.

❧

WHERE TO FIND OUT MORE ABOUT ESTHER FORBES

BOOKS

Silvey, Anita, ed. *The Essential Guide to Children's Books and Their Creators.* Boston: Houghton Mifflin Company, 2002.

Sutherland, Zena. *Children & Books.* 9th ed. New York: Addison Wesley Longman, 1997.

Vollstadt, Elizabeth Weiss. *Understanding Johnny Tremain.* San Diego: Lucent Books, 2001.

WEB SITE

WORCESTER AREA WRITERS
http://www.wpi.edu/Academics/Library/Archives/WAuthors/forbes/
To read a biography of Esther Forbes and to view photographs from her life

———

A MOVIE VERSION OF *JOHNNY TREMAIN* WAS RELEASED IN 1957.

Mem Fox

Born: March 5, 1946

Mem Fox has lived in many countries through-out the world. But as an adult, she returned to her native Australia. Many of her picture books for children show life in Australia. Her books also include themes about the importance of a strong family. Her more than thirty books for children have been published in many languages, including Indonesian, Chinese, Japanese, German, and Hebrew. Her best-known books include *Time for Bed, Hattie and the Fox, Koala Lou,* and *Night Noises.*

Mem Fox was born on March 5, 1946, in Melbourne, Australia. When she was only six months old, her family moved to the African

---

MEM FOX'S REAL NAME IS MERRION FRANCES FOX.

> *"I write for the child-within-the-parent who is reading to the child. I always write with adult readers in mind because my audience is often too young to read on their own."*

nation of Zimbabwe. Her missionary father had been sent to work in Africa. When she was old enough to go to school, Mem attended the mission school. She was the only white student there. After a year, she left to attend an all-white school in a nearby village.

Mem did not like how black people were treated in Africa. There was a great deal of racism in Zimbabwe and throughout Africa. When she finished high school, she decided to leave Africa. She moved to London, England, to attend Rose Bruford College, where she studied drama. Life in London was very different from what she was used to in Africa. She spent four years in London before graduating from college in 1968.

She married Malcolm Fox in 1969, and they lived in Africa briefly before moving to Australia in 1970. She taught drama at a college in Adelaide, Australia. During her career as a teacher, Fox also taught at other colleges and universities in Australia. She also went back to college in Australia to study children's literature.

FOX'S BOOK *TIME FOR BED* WAS NAMED TO OPRAH WINFREY'S LIST
OF THE TWENTY ALL-TIME BEST CHILDREN'S BOOKS.

A Selected Bibliography of Fox's Work

Particular Cow (2006)
Fairy, Fairy Quite Contrary (2005)
Where Is the Green Sheep? (2004)
The Magic Hat (2002)
Harriet, You'll Drive Me Wild (2000)
Sleepy Bears (1999)
Because of the Bloomers (1998)
Whoever You Are (1997)
A Bedtime Story (1996)
Feathers and Fools (1996)
Sophie (1994)
Time for Bed (1993)
Guess What? (1990)
Night Noises (1989)
Shoes from Grandpa (1989)
Koala Lou (1988)
With Love, at Christmas (1988)
Hattie and the Fox (1987)
Arabella: The Smallest Girl in the World (1986)
Wilfrid Gordon McDonald Partridge (1984)
Possum Magic (1983)

As an assignment for one of her children's literature classes, she wrote the draft of her first book, *Possum Magic*. She tried to get the book published, but it was rejected nine times in five years. She finally found a publisher who liked the book. Published in 1983, *Possum Magic* sold more than one million copies in its first ten years of publication. It is Australia's best-selling picture book.

> *"A five-hundred-word book takes me around two years to perfect. Only the best is good enough for kids. Only the best pays my mortgage."*

Along with her writing and teaching, Fox has worked on literacy, or teaching people to read. She has traveled all around the world giving speeches and workshops on literacy. She has received many awards for her work as a language arts expert as well as for her writing.

Mem Fox is retired from teaching, but she still travels as a literacy expert. She lives with her husband in Adelaide, Australia. She continues to write picture books for children.

WHERE TO FIND OUT MORE ABOUT MEM FOX

BOOKS

Fox, Mem. *Dear Mem Fox, I Have Read All Your Books, Even the Pathetic Ones: And Other Incidents in the Life of a Children's Book Author.* San Diego: Harcourt Brace Jovanovich, 1992.

McElmeel, Sharron L. *100 Most Popular Picture Book Authors and Illustrators: Biographical Sketches and Bibliographies.* Englewood, Colo.: Libraries Unlimited, 2000.

Mem's the Word. New York: Penguin, 1990.

Silvey, Anita, ed. *The Essential Guide to Children's Books and Their Creators.* Boston: Houghton Mifflin Company, 2002.

WEB SITE
MEM FOX HOME PAGE
http://www.memfox.net/
To read an autobiographical sketch by Mem Fox
and information about her books

MEM FOX'S FATHER'S NAME, WILFRID GORDON MCDONALD PARTRIDGE, IS ALSO THE TITLE OF HER SECOND BOOK. IN THE SAME BOOK, THERE IS A CHARACTER NAMED MISS NANCY—FOX'S MOTHER'S NAME!

Paula Fox

Born: April 22, 1923

Most writers will tell you that using your own life experiences to gather ideas for books is the best way to develop interesting stories. In the case of author Paula Fox, her life experiences have been so varied that it's no wonder she writes books full of truth and richness for adults and young readers.

Paula Fox was born on April 22, 1923, in New York City. Paula's

parents were more interested in their world travels than in being parents. After Paula was born, her father, a writer, and her mother left her at an orphanage. Although Paula did see her parents again, her contact with them was always brief.

Paula spent her early years living with a minister, whom she called Uncle Elwood, and his family in upstate New York. Uncle

IT TOOK PAULA FOX THREE MONTHS TO WRITE THE FIRST TEN PAGES OF *BORROWED FINERY: A MEMOIR.* SHE USED TO WRITE AN ENTIRE NOVEL FOR YOUNG READERS IN THAT TIME.

Elwood taught Paula to read and introduced her to libraries. The young girl was instantly spellbound by books. "Libraries meant freedom, solace, and truth to me," she says now. "Stories took me to other places. There was no television then, of course. Reading was everything to me."

Books and stories grounded Paula during the years she moved from place to place. At the age of six, Paula went to live with her grandmother in New York City. Her grandmother told stories of her youth in Spain. "Some of her tales were comic," Fox recalls, "and some were tales of dread."

> *"A lie hides the truth. A story tries to find it."*

THE VILLAGE BY THE SEA
Paula Fox

A Selected Bibliography of Fox's Work

Radiance Descending (1997)
The Eagle Kite (1995)
Western Wind (1993)
Monkey Island (1991)
The Village by the Sea (1988)
One-Eyed Cat (1984)
A Place Apart (1980)
The Slave Dancer (1973)
Blowfish Live in the Sea (1970)
Portrait of Ivan (1969)
The Stone-Faced Boy (1968)
How Many Miles to Babylon? (1967)
Maurice's Room (1966)

Fox's Major Literary Awards

1994 Boston Globe–Horn Book Fiction Honor Book
   Western Wind

1989 Boston Globe–Horn Book Fiction Award
   The Village by the Sea

1985 Newbery Honor Book
   One-Eyed Cat

1983 National Book Award
   A Place Apart

1978 Hans Christian Andersen Medal for Authors

1974 Newbery Medal
   The Slave Dancer

> *"No one can really explain what it is that drives them to write. It is simply a need. One of the nicest things about writing is that you make yourself laugh. You don't have to wait for a comedian to come along!"*

The following year, Paula joined her parents in California, but by the age of eight, she was separated from them again. She was sent to Cuba to live on a sugar plantation with relatives. Because she attended many schools in many different places, the library became the one constant in Paula's life.

By the age of sixteen, Paula Fox began working. Her first job was at the Warner Brothers movie studio in Hollywood, where she read novels written in English or Spanish to see if they would make good films. She later worked as a teacher, a salesperson, a model, and a lathe operator.

Paula Fox's first novel, *Poor George,* is for adults. It was published in 1967. She soon followed with a second novel called *Desperate Characters,* which was made into a movie in 1971.

Recalling her love of books as a child, Fox decided to try her hand at writing for young readers. Her first book for children was *Maurice's Room.* In 1973, she wrote *The Slave Dancer,* a historical novel about a boy who is kidnapped and put on a slave ship—and it won a Newbery Medal! Her other popular books for young readers include *Blowfish Live in the Sea; A Place Apart;* and *One-Eyed Cat.*

BECAUSE PAULA FOX MOVED A LOT AS A CHILD, BY THE TIME SHE WAS TWELVE YEARS OLD SHE HAD ATTENDED NINE DIFFERENT SCHOOLS.

At the age of seventy-six, Fox was attacked while strolling with her husband during a visit to Israel. She suffered head injuries and slight brain damage. After two years of therapy, during which time she struggled to regain her grasp of language, Paula Fox began writing again. The writing became an important part of her recovery, as a way back to normal life.

The result of this work is her memoir for adults, *Borrowed Finery: A Memoir,* in which she recounts the details of her amazing life. Fortunately, readers now get a chance to learn the true story of a writer whose real life is as interesting as any fiction she ever wrote.

❧

WHERE TO FIND OUT MORE ABOUT PAULA FOX

BOOKS

Drew, Bernard A. *The 100 Most Popular Young Adult Authors.* Englewood, Colo.: Libraries Unlimited, 1996.

Fox, Paula. *Borrowed Finery: A Memoir.* New York: Henry Holt, 2001.

McElmeel, Sharron L. *100 Most Popular Children's Authors: Biographical Sketches and Bibliographies.* Englewood, Colo.: Libraries Unlimited, 1999.

Silvey, Anita, ed. *The Essential Guide to Children's Books and Their Creators.* Boston: Houghton Mifflin, 2002.

Sutherland, Zena. *Children & Books.* 9th ed. New York: Addison Wesley Longman, 1997.

WEB SITE

RANDOM HOUSE: AUTHORS/ILLUSTRATORS
http://www.randomhouse.com/author/results.pperl?authorid=9127
To read an autobiographical sketch and booklist for Paula Fox

———

PAULA FOX BECAME FLUENT IN SPANISH DURING THE YEARS SHE ATTENDED A ONE-ROOM SCHOOLHOUSE WHILE LIVING ON A SUGAR PLANTATION IN CUBA.

Russell Freedman

Born: October 11, 1929

A newspaper article launched Russell Freedman on a career of writing books for young people. One day, while he was reading the *New York Times,* he noticed a story about a blind sixteen-year-old boy who had invented a Braille typewriter. (Braille is a system of printing for the blind. It uses raised dots that are "read" with the fingertips.) Freedman learned another interesting fact: more than 100 years earlier it was another blind sixteen-year-old, Louis Braille, who invented Braille.

Soon Freedman was at work on *Teenagers Who Made History.* The

book, published in 1961, told the story of young people who achieved great things. Freedman had discovered his vocation and has since written more than forty nonfiction books for children.

Freedman was born on October 11, 1929, in San Francisco, California. Books were an important part of his family life. His father was West Coast sales manager

RUSSELL FREEDMAN'S *LINCOLN: A PHOTOBIOGRAPHY* WAS THE FIRST NONFICTION BOOK TO WIN THE NEWBERY MEDAL IN THIRTY-TWO YEARS.

for a big publisher, and many famous authors came to dinner at his house.

After graduating from college in 1951, Freedman joined the U.S. Army and fought in the Korean War. When he returned home, he became a newspaper reporter. He also worked in public relations before turning to book writing.

"I don't know if I would ever want to write about someone I didn't admire. Writing a biography takes a year of my life. It means in a sense that I live with that person for a year."

Many of Freedman's first books were about animals. He discovered that photographs made his books stronger and clearer. So he learned how to research photos, sifting through as many as 1,000 pictures to find just the ones he wanted. He taught himself to write and plan books so that words and pictures worked together.

Then in 1980, he went to an exhibit of photographs of street children from the late nineteenth century. "What impressed me most of all was the way that those old photographs seemed to defy the passage of time," Freedman says. He took his editor to see the show. The result was *Immigrant Kids,* the first book in a new series of histories and biographies that Freedman wrote in the 1980s and 1990s.

Russell Freedman has written books about children in the Wild West, cowboys, and Indian chiefs. All of them are illustrated with

RUSSELL FREEDMAN DOESN'T LIKE TO BE CALLED A "NONFICTION WRITER." HE BELIEVES MANY PEOPLE THINK NONFICTION ISN'T AS IMPORTANT OR INTERESTING AS FICTION. FREEDMAN PREFERS TO BE CALLED A "FACTUAL AUTHOR."

A Selected Bibliography of Freedman's Work

Adventures of Marco Polo (2006)

Children of the Great Depression (2005)

The Voice That Changed a Nation: Marian Anderson and the Struggle for Equal Rights (2004)

In Defense of Liberty: The Story of America's Bill of Rights (2003)

Confucius: The Golden Rule (2002)

Martha Graham, a Dancer's Life (1998)

The Life and Death of Crazy Horse (1996)

Eleanor Roosevelt: A Life of Discovery (1993)

Franklin Delano Roosevelt (1990)

Buffalo Hunt (1988)

Lincoln: A Photobiography (1987)

Children of the Wild West (1983)

Immigrant Kids (1980)

Teenagers Who Made History (1961)

Freedman's Select Major Literary Awards

2006 Orbis Pictus Award
   Children of the Great Depression

2005 Newbery Honor Book
2005 Orbis Pictus Honor Book
   The Voice That Changed a Nation: Marian Anderson and the Struggle for Equal Rights

2004 Orbis Pictus Honor Book
   In Defense of Liberty: The Story of America's Bill of Rights

2003 Orbis Pictus Honor Book
   Confucius: The Golden Rule

1998 Boston Globe–Horn Book Nonfiction Honor Book
   Martha Graham, a Dancer's Life

1998 Laura Ingalls Wilder Award

1997 Carter G. Woodson Honor Book
1997 Orbis Pictus Honor Book
   The Life and Death of Crazy Horse

1994 Boston Globe–Horn Book Nonfiction Award
1994 Newbery Honor Book
   Eleanor Roosevelt: A Life of Discovery

1991 Orbus Pictus Award
   Franklin Delano Roosevelt

1989 Carter G. Woodson Outstanding Merit Book
   Buffalo Hunt

1988 Newbery Medal
   Lincoln: A Photobiography

1984 *Boston Globe–Horn Book* Nonfiction Honor Book
   Children of the Wild West

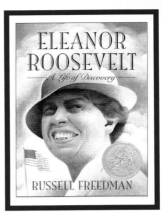

historical photos and show readers what life was really like for people in the past.

In time, Freedman turned his attention to individual people, creating a kind of book he called "photobiography." His best-known photobiography is of U.S. president Abraham Lincoln. To write it, Freedman studied letters Lincoln had written and received and pored over historical photos. He visited places where Lincoln had lived—and the place where he died.

More photobiographies followed. Freedman feels the people he writes about have messages for readers about how to live life. "If you want to know who my heroes are, take a look at my books. I was drawn to Eleanor Roosevelt because

> *"Isn't it more encouraging for a young reader to know that others, even the great figures of history, have shared the doubts and fears a child feels, than to be confronted with a paragon?"*

of the quality of her heart; to Crazy Horse because of his courage and his uncompromising integrity; to Abraham Lincoln because of his spirit of forgiveness," Freedman says.

❧

WHERE TO FIND OUT MORE ABOUT RUSSELL FREEDMAN

BOOKS

McElmeel, Sharron L. *100 Most Popular Children's Authors: Biographical Sketches and Bibliographies.*. Englewood, Colo.: Libraries Unlimited, 1999.

Silvey, Anita, ed. *The Essential Guide to Children's Books and Their Creators.* Boston: Houghton Mifflin, 2002.

WEB SITE

HOUGHTON MIFFLIN: MEET THE AUTHOR
http://www.eduplace.com/kids/hmr/mtai/freedman.html
To read a biographical sketch and booklist for Russell Freedman

ONE OF FREEDMAN'S FAVORITE BOOKS, HENDRIK WILLEM VAN LOON'S *THE STORY OF MANKIND,* WON THE VERY FIRST NEWBERY MEDAL. "I THINK IT WAS THE FIRST BOOK THAT GAVE ME A SENSE OF HISTORY AS A LIVING THING," FREEDMAN SAYS.

Don Freeman

Born: August 11, 1908
Died: February 1, 1978

s a little boy, Don Freeman loved to draw. But his career as an artist almost never happened. In fact, Freeman's first job was as a trumpet player!

Don Freeman was born on August 11, 1908, in San Diego, California. Because his parents were not able to care for their children, Don and his older brother, Warren, lived with a guardian named Mrs. Blass in Chula Vista, about 11 miles away from San Diego. Don Freeman's father remained in San Diego, where he worked in a clothing store. He visited his sons every Sunday and often brought Don art materials.

CORDUROY HAS APPEARED IN AN ANIMATED TELEVISION
SERIES AND SEVERAL VIDEOS.

A few years later, the Freeman boys were able to join their father in San Diego. Mrs. Blass came along to care for Don and Warren. Don spent many hours in the clothing store where his father worked. He enjoyed sketching the customers. In the evening, Don and his father often went to the theater. Don Freeman also loved music. For his tenth birthday, his father gave him a trumpet. Don taught himself to play by listening to records.

After he graduated from high school, Freeman took art

"Creating picture books for children fulfills all my enthusiasms and interests and love of life."

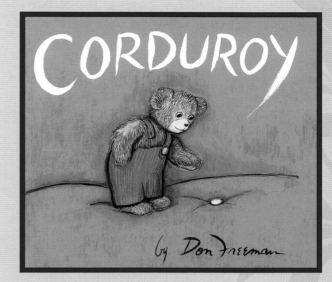

A Selected Bibliography of Freeman's Work

A Pocket for Corduroy (1978)
Bearymore (1976)
The Paper Party: Story and Pictures (1974)
Tilly Witch (1969)
Corduroy (1968)
Best Friends (Illustrations only, 1967)
Dandelion (1964)
Norman the Doorman (1959)
Space Witch (1959)
Fly High, Fly Low (1957)
Ghost Town Treasure (Illustrations only, 1957)
Mop Top (1955)
Beady Bear: Story and Pictures (1954)
Pet of the Met (1953)
Chuggy and the Blue Caboose (1951)

Freeman's Major Literary Award

1958 Caldecott Honor Book
Fly High, Fly Low

classes at the San Diego School of Fine Arts. In 1929, he hitchhiked across the country to New York City. To support himself, he played the trumpet that his father had given him years before. Freeman also studied at New York's Art Students League and spent hours walking around the city and sketching the people and things he saw.

In 1930, Freeman's musical career ended when he accidentally left his trumpet on the subway. Freeman began drawing for several New York City newspapers and magazines. In 1931, he married Lydia Cooley, an

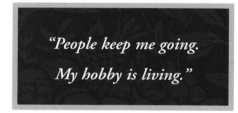

"People keep me going. My hobby is living."

artist he had met at the San Diego School of Fine Arts. The couple later had a son named Roy Warren. During the 1940s, Freeman illustrated several books for adults. He also published *It Shouldn't Happen,* a book of cartoons based on his experiences in the U.S. Army. In 1949, the Freeman family moved to Santa Barbara, California. Then Freeman and his wife wrote and illustrated their first children's book, *Chuggy and the Blue Caboose,* which was published in 1951.

After creating Chuggy, Freeman focused on writing and illustrating books for children. His second book, *Pet of the Met,* won the Book World Children's Spring Book Festival Award in 1953. In 1958, *Fly High, Fly Low* was named a Caldecott Honor Book.

CHUGGY AND THE BLUE CABOOSE WAS ORIGINALLY WRITTEN FOR
FREEMAN'S YOUNG SON. A LOCAL LIBRARIAN SAW THE BOOK AND
SUGGESTED THE FREEMANS SEND IT TO A PUBLISHER.

Freeman's most popular creation was a little bear in green overalls named Corduroy. Since its publication in 1968, *Corduroy* has become a classic children's book. Another book about Corduroy, *A Pocket for Corduroy,* was published in 1978, shortly after Freeman's death.

Don Freeman died on February 1, 1978, at the age of sixty-nine. Freeman's books have been translated into many foreign languages, and more than one million copies of his books are in print. They continue to delight children all over the world.

❧

WHERE TO FIND OUT MORE ABOUT DON FREEMAN

BOOKS

Children's Literature Review, vol. 30. Gale, 1993.

Silvey, Anita, ed. *The Essential Guide to Children's Books and Their Creators.* Boston: Houghton Mifflin, 2002.

Something about the Author. Autobiography Series. Vol. 17. Detroit: Gale Research, 1979.

WEB SITES

PENGUIN GROUP
http://us.penguingroup.com/nf/Author/AuthorPage/0,,0_1000011252,00.html
To read about Don Freeman

SULLIVAN GOSS: DON FREEMAN
http://www.sullivangoss.com/DonFreeman
To read a biography of Don Freeman as well as to learn more about his paintings and illustrations

---

ALTHOUGH FREEMAN LIVED IN A RURAL AREA OF CALIFORNIA, HE LOVED BIG CITIES.

Jean Fritz

Born: November 16, 1915

Jean Fritz loves history. She is considered one of the best authors of historical fiction for children and young adults. She has written more than fifty picture books, biographies, and novels during her long career. Her most famous and popular books include *The Double Life of Pocahontas, And Then What Happened, Paul Revere?* and *Where Do You Think You're Going, Christopher Columbus?*

Jean Fritz was born on November 16, 1915, in Hankow, China. Her parents worked as missionaries, and she lived in China until she was about thirteen years old. As a young girl, Jean knew she wanted to be a writer. She wrote about her thoughts, ideas, and emotions in a journal.

As she grew up, Jean's parents told her stories about life in America. Her father also

---

FRITZ FOUNDED THE JEAN FRITZ WRITER'S WORKSHOPS AND TAUGHT WRITING FROM 1961 TO 1969.

told her stories about American heroes. These stories made Jean want to move to the United States. "I think it is because I was so far away that I developed a homesickness that made me want to embrace not just a given part of America at a given time but the whole of it," Fritz says.

> *"I get letters from readers sometimes who say they like the way I add 'fun' to history. I don't add anything. It's all true, because past times were just as filled with exciting events and 'fun' stories as are present times."*

In time, Jean Fritz's family moved back to the United States. She received a degree from Wheaton College and attended Columbia University. She began her career working as a research assistant at a publishing company and as a children's librarian. She also worked as a writing teacher throughout her career.

> *"The question I am most often asked is 'How do I find my ideas?' The answer is, I don't. Ideas find me. A character in history will suddenly step right out of the past and demand a book."*

Fritz published her first book, *Bunny Hopwell's First Spring,* in 1954. She soon published *The Cabin Faced West,* the first of several historical fiction books she has written.

JEAN FRITZ HAS WRITTEN SHORT STORIES FOR *SEVENTEEN,* *REDBOOK,* AND THE *NEW YORKER.*

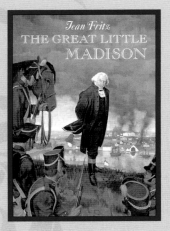

A Selected Bibliography of Fritz's Work

The Great Little Madison (1989)
Shh! We're Writing the Constitution (1987)
The Double Life of Pocahontas (1983)
Homesick: My Own Story (1982)
Where Do You Think You're Going, Christopher Columbus? (1980)
Stonewall (1979)
Will You Sign Here, John Hancock? (1976)
Why Don't You Get a Horse, Sam Adams? (1974)
And Then What Happened, Paul Revere? (1973)
The Cabin Faced West (1958)
Bunny Hopwell's First Spring (1954)

Fritz's Major Literary Awards

1990 Boston Globe-Horn Book Nonfiction Award
1990 Orbis Pictus Award
  The Great Little Madison

1986 Laura Ingalls Wilder Award

1984 Boston Globe-Horn Book Nonfiction Award
  The Double Life of Pocahontas

1983 Boston Globe-Horn Book Fiction Honor Book
1983 National Book Award
1983 Newbery Honor Book
  Homesick: My Own Story

1980 Boston Globe-Horn Book Nonfiction Honor Book
  Stonewall

1976 Boston Globe-Horn Book Nonfiction Honor Book
  Will You Sign Here, John Hancock?

1974 Boston Globe-Horn Book Fiction Honor Book
  And Then What Happened, Paul Revere?

Fritz wants to make the characters come alive in her historical fiction books. She does a great deal of research for each of her books. "I like being a detective, a treasure hunter, an eavesdropper," Fritz explains. "I look for personalities whose lives make good stories." In writing her books, she refuses to use fictional dialogue for her characters. The words spoken and written by the characters in her books are taken from letters, journals, diaries, and other sources. Fritz believes that the original words make the books more real and interesting.

She has written about many people from U.S. history including George Washington, Paul Revere, Patrick Henry, and John

Hancock. Her books have also described events such as the writing of the U.S. Constitution, the Revolutionary War, and the arrival of the Pilgrims at Plymouth Rock.

Fritz lives on the Hudson River in Dobbs Ferry, New York. Her two children are now grown and live near her home. She continues to write for children and young adults.

❧

WHERE TO FIND OUT MORE ABOUT JEAN FRITZ

BOOKS

Fritz, Jean. *China Homecoming*. New York: G. P. Putnam's Sons, 1985.

Fritz, Jean. *Homesick: My Own Story*. Waterville, Me.: Thorndike Press, 2001.

Fritz, Jean. *Surprising Myself*. Katonah, N.Y.: R. C. Owen Publishers, 1992.

McElmeel, Sharron L. *100 Most Popular Children's Authors: Biographical Sketches and Bibliographies.*. Englewood, Colo.: Libraries Unlimited, 1999.

Silvey, Anita, ed. *The Essential Guide to Children's Books and Their Creators*. Boston: Houghton Mifflin, 2002.

WEB SITES

CAROL HURST'S CHILDREN'S LITERATURE SITE
http://www.carolhurst.com/authors/jfritz.html
To read a biographical sketch of Jean Fritz and descriptions of some of her books

HOUGHTON MIFFLIN READING: MEET JAN FRITZ
http://www.eduplace.com/kids/hmr/mtai/fritz.html
To read an autobiographical sketch by Jean Fritz

———

IN DOING RESEARCH FOR A BOOK, FRITZ OFTEN TRAVELS TO WHERE HER SUBJECT WAS BORN OR ONCE LIVED. THESE TRIPS HELP HER TO LEARN MORE ABOUT THE PEOPLE SHE IS WRITING ABOUT.

Cornelia Funke

Born: December 10, 1958

I t's no wonder that Cornelia Funke's fantasy novels are so popular. She leads young readers into magical, mysterious worlds where children have amazing, hair-raising adventures.

Cornelia was born in 1958 in Dorsten, a little town in Westphalia, Germany. As a child, she enjoyed playing outdoors and hearing her grandmother tell stories. Her father often took her to the library, and she loved being around lots of books. She also liked drawing.

At Saint Ursula Grammar School, Cornelia enjoyed writing essays, although hers were always too long and often wandered from the topic. As a child, she never thought about becoming an author. Instead, she had a variety of adventurous plans, such as becoming an astronaut or marrying a Native American tribal chief.

TIME MAGAZINE LISTED FUNKE AMONG THE ONE HUNDRED MOST INFLUENTIAL PEOPLE OF 2005.

After completing secondary school, Cornelia moved to Hamburg, Germany, to attend the University of Hamburg. She knew she wanted to work with children, so she earned a degree related to education. While in college, she met a book printer named Rolf Funke. The couple were married and later had two children—Anna and Ben.

After graduation, Funke spent three years as a social worker, helping troubled children. Thanks to her job, she

> *"The children always ask: when are you going to stop writing? And I say: when I drop dead. I can't live without writing. It's my obsession."*

A Selected Bibliography of Funke's Work

Inkspell (2007)
Ghosthunters and the Incredibly Revolting Ghost (2006)
Inkheart (2005)
Pirate Girl (2005)
Dragon Rider (2004)
The Princess Knight (2004)
The Thief Lord (2002)

learned about the kinds of books that grab kids' imaginations. This shaped her ideas about the books she would later write. While working, Funke completed a course in book illustration at Hamburg State College of Design. Then she began illustrating children's books.

Many of the stories Funke was illustrating called for pictures of children in everyday situations. But she really preferred drawing dragons, sea serpents, and other fantastic creatures. She didn't like the stories she was illustrating either. Funke had always enjoyed fantasies such as J. R. R. Tolkien's Lord of the Rings and C. S. Lewis's Chronicles of Narnia. She finally decided to write her own fantasy stories so she could draw whatever she wanted.

> *"I love to imagine riding on dragons or meeting creatures I have never met before and make them feel real for my readers."*

Funke began writing and illustrating her own books when she was twenty-eight. Since then, she has become one of Germany's most popular children's authors. She has written more than forty books, ranging from picture books for young children to novels for older readers.

Funke's books have been translated into more than twenty languages. But readers in the United States weren't introduced to her work until 2002. That was the year her fantasy story *Herr der Diebe* was published

———

FUNKE'S BOOKS *THE THIEF LORD*, *INKHEART*, AND *DRAGON RIDER* ARE BEING MADE INTO MOVIES.

in English as *The Thief Lord*. This tale follows a band of runaway children who have dangerous and magical adventures. *The Thief Lord* was an immediate best seller. So were Funke's subsequent English-language titles, including *Inkheart*, *Dragon Rider*, and *Inkspell*.

Funke does extensive research for each of her books. Then she outlines the plot. After about six months of preparation, she begins to write. As she writes, she makes pen-and-ink sketches of her characters. She has even illustrated several of her novels. She writes in German, and the books are then translated into other languages.

Funke and her family lived in Hamburg until 2005. Now they make their home near Los Angeles, California.

❧

WHERE TO FIND OUT MORE ABOUT CORNELIA FUNKE

WEB SITES

KIDS READS
http://www.kidsreads.com/authors/au-funke-cornelia.asp
For a biography of the author

THE WORLD OF CORNELIA FUNKE
http://www.cornelia-funke.de/en/
To read about the author on her Web site

FUNKE COLLECTS STUFFED DRAGONS.

Wanda Gág

Born: March 11, 1893
Died: June 27, 1946

Children have enjoyed Wanda Gág's illustrated books for more than seventy years. Her beloved classic, *Millions of Cats*, has been called the first modern picture book for children.

Wanda Hazel Gág was born in New Ulm, Minnesota, in 1893 and was the oldest of seven children. Her father and maternal grandparents were immigrants from Bohemia, a region in today's Czech Republic. The children listened for hours as their grandmother, aunts, and uncles told them German folktales. Only German was spoken in her home, so Wanda did not begin speaking English until she went to school.

Wanda's father, a painter who decorated houses and churches, encouraged all the children to draw and paint. Sadly, he died of tuberculosis when Wanda was fifteen. Because her mother was not well,

PEOPLE CAN VISIT GÁG'S CHILDHOOD HOME AT **226 NORTH WASHINGTON STREET IN NEW ULM.**

Wanda took care of the family. The Gágs had little to eat, and they wore clothes donated from local charities. Some friends urged Wanda to quit school and get a job. Others suggested putting the younger children in an orphanage. But Wanda was determined to keep the family together and to make sure all her siblings got an education. She worked hard on her writing and art skills, and her first stories and drawings were published in the *Minneapolis Junior Journal* in Minneapolis, Minnesota.

> *"I have more courage and self-assurance than many a man, and yet I am treated as a mere wisp of femininity."*

After graduating from New Ulm High School in 1912, Gág worked for a year as a schoolteacher. In 1913, she won a scholarship to Saint Paul Institute of Arts in Saint Paul, Minnesota. Then, with financial help from friends, she attended Minneapolis School of Art from 1914 to 1917.

> *"The strain of expressing other people's ideas, when my own were clamoring for attention, became too great."*

Gág moved to New York City in 1917 to study at the Art Students' League. Over the next few years, she continued supporting her family by working as a commercial artist. She very much wanted to work on her

GÁG ILLUSTRATED HER FIRST CHILDREN'S BOOK IN 1917. IT WAS A BOOK THAT USED MOTHER GOOSE RHYMES TO TEACH PUNCTUATION AND CAPITALIZATION.

A Selected Bibliography of Gág's Work

Nothing at All (1941)

Snow White and the Seven Dwarfs (1938)

Tales from Grimm (1936)

Gone Is Gone; or, The Story of a Man Who Wanted to Do Housework (1935)

The ABC Bunny (1933)

Snippy and Snappy (1931)

The Funny Thing (1929)

Millions of Cats (1928)

Gág's Major Literary Awards

1942 Caldecott Honor Book
 Nothing At All

1939 Caldecott Honor Book
 Snow White and the Seven Dwarfs

1934 Newbery Honor Book
 The ABC Bunny

1929 Newbery Honor Book
 Millions of Cats

own art, though, so she bought a country home in Connecticut. There she developed her art style by drawing and painting her surroundings.

In 1926, Gág was invited to hold a one-woman art show in New York City. This brought her to the attention of a book publisher, who asked Gág to submit an illustrated children's book. It was *Millions of Cats*, a story about an elderly couple trying to choose just one pet cat among millions. First published in 1928, this would remain her most famous work.

Soon Gág and her close companion, Earle Humphreys, bought a farm they named All Creation, near Milford, New Jersey. In this pleasant country setting, Gág went on to write several other books that proved popular. She also translated and illustrated dozens of tales by Jacob and Wilhelm Grimm.

Gág produced art using many different techniques, including pen-and-ink drawings, watercolors, and oil paintings. She is especially known for her lithograph prints, which she made by carving an image onto stone or metal.

Gág and Humphreys finally married in 1943. She died three years later at the age of fifty-three.

❧

WHERE TO FIND OUT MORE ABOUT WANDA GÁG

BOOKS

Hoyle, Karen Nelson. *Wanda Gág*. New York: Twayne Publishers, 1994.

McElmeel, Sharron L. *100 Most Popular Picture Book Authors and Illustrators: Biographical Sketches and Bibliographies*. Englewood, Colo.: Libraries Unlimited, 2000.

Silvey, Anita, ed. *The Essential Guide to Children's Books and Their Creators*. Boston: Houghton Mifflin Company, 2002.

WEB SITES

CHILDREN'S LITERATURE NETWORK
http://www.childrensliteraturenetwork.org/events/destins/gaghouse.html
To read a biography and find out about visiting the family home in Minnesota

WOMEN CHILDREN'S BOOK ILLUSTRATORS
http://www.ortakales.com/illustrators/Gag.HTML
To read a extensive biography of Wanda Gág and connect to additional sites

———

GÁG SOMETIMES PAINTED DIRECTLY ONTO SANDPAPER, TO CREATE A PICTURE WITH AN INTERESTING TEXTURE.

Paul Galdone

Born: 1907
Died: November 7, 1986

Few people will ever be able to match the work of Paul Galdone. As an illustrator and writer of children's books, he completed almost 300 books during his lifetime.

Paul Galdone was born in Budapest, Hungary, in 1907. He was just a teenager when he moved to the United States in 1921. Eventually, Galdone got the chance to study art. He studied with other young

artists at the Art Students League in New York City. Then Galdone enrolled at the New York School of Industrial Design.

When Paul Galdone finished his studies, he began his career in the art department of a book publisher in New York City. He used the skills he learned there for the rest of his life. Galdone learned how artists, authors, and editors work together, how pages are laid out, and how books are produced.

PAUL GALDONE ILLUSTRATED A WIDE VARIETY OF BOOKS, INCLUDING A BOOK OF KNOCK-KNOCK JOKES AND A STORY FROM THE BIBLE.

At his job, Galdone designed and illustrated book covers and dust jackets, many of them for adult readers. His cover illustrations appeared on books by Mark Twain, Jane Austen, Edgar Allan Poe, and Charles Dickens. For this work, he used bold lettering and dramatic images very different from his children's illustrations.

During World War II (1939–1945), Paul Galdone

A Selected Bibliography of Galdone's Work

Nursery Classics: A Golden Treasury (2001)

Cat Goes Fiddle-I-Fee (1985)

Rumpelstiltskin (1985)

The Elves and the Shoemaker (1984)

The Monster and the Tailor: A Ghost Story (1982)

The Turtle and the Monkey (1983)

Insects All around Us (Illustrations only, 1981)

King of the Cats: A Ghost Story (1980)

Anatole and the Pied Piper (Illustrations only, 1979)

Zed and the Monsters (Illustrations only, 1979)

Puss in Boots (1976)

The Gingerbread Boy (1975)

The Queen Who Couldn't Bake Gingerbread (Illustrations only, 1975)

The Three Billy Goats Gruff (Illustrations only, 1973)

Basil and the Pygmy Cats; a Basil of Baker Street Mystery (Illustrations only, 1971)

Anatole and the Thirty Thieves (Illustrations only, 1969)

The Hairy Horror Trick (Illustrations only, 1969)

Whiskers, My Cat (Illustrations only, 1967)

The Hare and the Tortoise (Illustrations only, 1962)

The Disappearing Dog Trick (Illustrations only, 1961)

Old Mother Hubbard and Her Dog (Illustrations only, 1960)

Bascombe, the Fastest Hound Alive (Illustrations only, 1958)

Anatole and the Cat (Illustrations only, 1957)

Anatole (Illustrations only, 1956)

Nine Lives; or, the Celebrated Cat of Beacon Hill (Illustrations only, 1951)

Galdone's Major Literary Awards

1958 Caldecott Honor Book
  Anatole and the Cat

1957 Caldecott Honor Book
  Anatole

> *"What will you give me," said the little man, "if I spin this straw into gold for you?"*
> —*from* **Rumpelstiltskin**

worked in the art department of the U.S. Army Corps of Engineers. After his military service, Galdone began illustrating books for children.

For children just beginning to read, Galdone illustrated the Anatole and Basil books, both written by Eve Titus. Anatole is a French mouse who cleverly solves problems faced by his mouse friends. Basil is a British mouse who solves mysteries. Galdone's charming mouse pictures are in black and white, with the occasional one or two colors added.

Galdone also illustrated many books for older children. Among his most popular books are those relating the adventures of Kerby Maxwell. Books written by Scott Corbett such as *The Hairy Horror Trick* and *The Disappearing Dog Trick* include many pen-and-ink illustrations of Kerby and his friend Fenton.

Throughout his life, Paul Galdone had a special interest in fables. He gathered tales from around the world, and then retold and illustrated them. He published stories from Germany, Russia, India, Puerto Rico, and the Philippines. One such story is *The Turtle and the Monkey*. This fable tells of a turtle who needs help getting a banana tree out of the river. She succeeds in getting the monkey to help her but comes to regret his

PAUL GALDONE HELD MANY JOBS DURING HIS LIFE. EARLY POSITIONS INCLUDED BUS BOY, ELECTRICIAN'S HELPER, AND FUR DRYER!

assistance when he grows greedy and asks for more fruit than he deserves. He also retold and illustrated tales from the Brothers Grimm, Hans Christian Andersen, and Aesop. Galdone's exciting pictures bring to life ancient fables such as Aesop's *The Hare and the Tortoise.* This story explains how a slow but determined tortoise wins the race over the quick but foolish hare.

> *"Today I brew, tomorrow I bake. The next day, the young Queen's child I'll take. Soon far and wide will spread the fame that Rumpelstiltskin is my name."*
> —*from* **Rumpelstiltskin**

Paul Galdone enjoyed illustrating for people of all ages. He died of a heart attack on November 7, 1986, leaving behind a collection of work that children and adults will enjoy for years to come.

❧

WHERE TO FIND OUT MORE ABOUT PAUL GALDONE

BOOKS

Collier, Laurie, and Joyce Nakamura, eds. *Major Authors and Illustrators for Children and Young Adults: A Selection of Sketches from Something about the Author.* Detroit: Gale Research, 1993.

McElmeel, Sharron L. *100 Most Popular Picture Book Authors and Illustrators: Biographical Sketches and Bibliographies..* Englewood, Colo.: Libraries Unlimited, 2000.

WEB SITE

HOUGHTON MIFFLIN
http://www.houghtonmifflinbooks.com/catalog/authordetail.cfm?authorID=3709
To read a biographical sketch about Paul Galdone

Jack Gantos

Born: July 2, 1951

Jack Gantos became interested in becoming a writer by writing in a diary. At first, he wrote in a diary because that's what his sister did. She was older, and he liked to imitate her. Over time, Gantos began using his diary to keep track of things that were important to him. This interest in writing was enough to help Gantos begin his career as a writing teacher and children's author. He is best known as the author of the Rotten Ralph series. He has also written other picture books for children, as well as novels for young people.

Jack Gantos was born on July 2, 1951, in Mount Pleasant, Pennsylvania. Jack was in second grade when he told his mother he wanted

---

MANY OF THE ROTTEN RALPH BOOKS HAVE BEEN PUBLISHED IN
HEBREW AND JAPANESE.

a diary like his sister. His mother finally agreed to get him a diary. She told him that he had to write in it every day. He would sit next to his sister and write in his diary. He would also try to peek at what his sister was writing. "When she caught me, she just laughed," Gantos says. " 'Go ahead and look,' she said and showed me her diary." He could not read what his sister had written because she wrote in French!

A few years later, Jack's family was planning to move to Barbados, an island in the Caribbean Sea. Jack's mother told him that

> *"I still read and write in my journal every day."*

he could only bring his books and diaries when they moved. He did not know what to do because he had collected many baseball cards, stamps, marbles, rocks, and butterflies that he wanted to keep. Jack figured out ways to put many of these things in his diaries. "By the time we were ready to move, I had put all of my junk into all of my diaries," Gantos says. "My mother was very surprised, but because my junk was now so well organized, she let me bring it."

Jack Gantos continued writing in his journals through high school and college. When he was a student at Emerson College in Boston, he met an art student who did illustrations. Gantos decided to begin writing children's books.

GANTOS ATTENDED TEN DIFFERENT SCHOOLS WHEN HE WAS GROWING UP.

A Selected Bibliography of Gantos's Work

Love Curse of the Rumbaughs (2006)

Best in Show for Rotten Ralph (2005)

Hole in My Life (2002)

Practice Makes Perfect for Rotten Ralph (2002)

What Would Joey Do? (2002)

Rotten Ralph Helps Outs (2001)

Joey Pigza Loses Control (2000)

Wedding Bells for Rotten Ralph (1999)

Back to School for Rotten Ralph (1998)

Joey Pigza Swallowed the Key (1998)

Rotten Ralph's Halloween Howl (1998)

Desire Lines (1997)

Jack's Black Book (1997)

Rotten Ralph's Rotten Romance (1997)

Jack's New Power: Stories from a Caribbean Year (1995)

Heads or Tails: Stories from the Sixth Grade (1994)

Not So Rotten Ralph (1994)

Happy Birthday, Rotten Ralph (1990)

Rotten Ralph's Show and Tell (1989)

Rotten Ralph's Trick or Treat! (1986)

Swampy Alligator (1980)

The Werewolf Family (1980)

Willy's Raiders (1980)

The Perfect Pal (1979)

Worse Than Rotten, Ralph (1978)

Fair-Weather Friends (1977)

Sleepy Ronald (1976)

Rotten Ralph (1976)

Gantos's Major Literary Awards

2003 Michael L. Printz Honor Book
  Hole in My Life

2001 Newbery Honor Book
  Joey Pigza Loses Control

The first book Gantos wrote was rejected because the publisher said it was boring. But then Gantos remembered that a teacher once told him to write about things that were familiar. "I looked down at the floor and saw my lousy, grumpy, hissing creep of a cat that loved to scratch my ankles, throw fur around the house, and shred my clothes in my closet," Gantos says. The cat was the inspiration for his first children's book,

Rotten Ralph, published in 1976. He went on to write many more books in the Rotten Ralph series.

Along with writing for children, Gantos teaches courses in children's book writing at Vermont College. He also travels around the country to speak at schools, libraries, and writing conferences.

"I enjoy my work as much as possible. I read good books and I want to write good books."

◈

WHERE TO FIND OUT MORE ABOUT JACK GANTOS

BOOKS

Gantos, Jack. *Hole in My Life.* New York: Farrar, Straus, and Giroux, 2002.

Silvey, Anita, ed. *The Essential Guide to Children's Books and Their Creators.* Boston: Houghton Mifflin, 2002.

WEB SITES

JACK GANTOS HOME PAGE
http://www.jackgantos.com/
For the author's Web page featuring works, biographical information, and photos

KIDSREADS.COM
http://www.kidsreads.com/reviews/0374399891.asp
To read a synopsis and review for Newbery
Honor Book *Joey Pigza Loses Control*

LD ONLINE: EXCLUSIVE INTERVIEW WITH JACK GANTOS
http://www.ldonline.org/kidzone/books_excerpt/joey_key_interview.html
To read an interview with Jack Gantos and excerpts
from *Joey Pigza Swallowed the Key*

———

IN THE NOVEL *HEADS OR TAILS: STORIES FROM THE SIXTH GRADE,* GANTOS TALKS
ABOUT GROWING UP WITH HIS SISTER AND MOVING WITH HIS FAMILY.

Carmen Lomas Garza

Born: 1948

Carmen Lomas Garza grew up in Kingsville, Texas, not far from the Mexican border. As a child, she was fortunate to have many relatives living in the area. Aunts, uncles, and cousins were often around the house. They chatted, cooked, ate, and played with Carmen and her brothers and sisters. The relatives told wonderful stories about their Indian, Texan, Mexican, and Spanish ancestors. They told Carmen stories about her grandparents and great-grandparents.

Carmen Lomas Garza was born in 1948. Her mother was a self-taught artist. She often painted small pictures for *lotería* cards. They were like bingo cards but with tiny pictures instead of numbers. Carmen's mother would paint the little pictures with ink and watercolor while

---

GARZA MADE A HUGE CUTOUT OF HER GRANDFATHER WATERING CORN.
IT IS FIVE FEET TALL AND EIGHT FEET WIDE!

Carmen watched in wonder. Carmen thought what her mother did was magic. Even then, she thought she might like to be a painter one day.

Carmen started saving the notebook paper she used at school. The back of the paper was blank and perfect for drawing. She spent hours and hours drawing on the backs of the sheets. She drew all kinds of things—hands and feet, people sleeping, pets, pictures in magazines. She took her first art classes in grade school. By the time she was thirteen, she knew for sure that she wanted to be an artist.

In high school, Carmen took more art classes. She loved them. Her teacher noticed how

> *"I always wanted to do artwork in color because I remember in color. I remember the clothing in color, the lighting, the walls—you know, just everything in color."*

hard Carmen worked and helped her get a college scholarship. She began studying art at Texas A&I University (now Texas A&M University) in Kingsville right after finishing high school.

Garza always liked to learn from other artists. She often visited other Mexican American artists to see what they were doing. One time she was visiting some other artists and saw a book on Mexican folk art that explained how to do cut-paper art called *papel picado*.

A 1991 EXHIBIT OF GARZA'S WORK IN AUSTIN, TEXAS, DREW MORE THAN ONE THOUSAND VISITORS ON THE FIRST DAY!

MAGIC
WINDOWS
Ventanas mágicas

CARMEN LOMAS GARZA

A Selected Bibliography of Garza's Work

Magic Windows/Ventanas mágicas (1999)

Making Magic Windows: Creating Papel Picado/Cut-Paper Art with Carmen Lomas Garza (1999)

In My Family/En mi familia (1996)

Family Pictures/Cuadros de familia (1990)

Garza's Major Literary Awards

2000 Carter G. Woodson Honor Book
2000 Pura Belpré Award for Illustration
   Magic Windows/Ventanas mágicas

1998 Pura Belpré Honor Book for Illustration
   In My Family/En mi familia

1996 Pura Belpré Honor Book for Illustration
   Family Pictures/Cuadros de familia

Garza gave paper cutting a try and loved it. She started making cutouts of all kinds of designs and images. In time, her cutouts became more and more complex. Some cutouts were pictures from her childhood. They showed her mother making tortillas, family members making paper flowers, and her grandfather trimming a cactus. Garza's book *Magic Windows/Ventanas mágicas* has some of her cutouts, along with English and Spanish explanations. In *Making Magic*

"When I was growing up, I was very shy and I didn't speak very much. I didn't learn to speak out until I was in college. My artwork helped me do that."

Windows: Creating Papel Picado/Cut-Paper Art with Carmen Lomas Garza, Garza explains how to make tissue-paper cutouts called *banderitas.* Garza likes to teach her nieces and nephews this ancient art because she believes this helps connect them to their ancestors.

Garza's paintings also show her memories of daily life in Kingsville. Her book *In My Family/En mi familia* has paintings of a wedding day, a local dance, and people just sitting on the front porch. Another book, *Family Pictures/Cuadros de familia* shows everyday scenes from her childhood. Her brightly colored pictures show how friends and family have always been important in her life.

❧

WHERE TO FIND OUT MORE ABOUT CARMEN LOMAS GARZA

BOOK
Rockman, Connie C., ed. *Eighth Book of Junior Authors and Illustrators.* New York: H. W. Wilson Company, 2000.

WEB SITES
CARMEN LOMAS GARZA'S HOME PAGE
http://www.carmenlomasgarza.com
To read a biographical sketch of Carmen Lomas Garza, information about her books, and answers to frequently asked questions

LEGACY: A LATINO BICENTENNIAL REFLECTION
http://www.esperanto.com/Legacy/CLGarza.html
A biographical sketch of the illustrator and her work titled, Tamalada

---

IT TAKES GARZA SEVERAL YEARS TO FINISH PAINTING EACH BOOK. SHE USUALLY NEEDS FROM THREE TO NINE MONTHS FOR EACH PAINTING!

Jean Craighead George

Born: July 2, 1919

It is sometimes hard for readers to name their favorite book by Jean Craighead George because there are so many. For more than fifty years, George has been writing stories for children. She and her books have won many awards. One book, *My Side of the Mountain,* was even made into a movie.

Jean Craighead George was born on July 2, 1919, in Washington, D.C. Her father was an entomologist. He studied bugs. Jean's brothers, mother, and other relatives also studied nature.

Jean's family loved the outdoors and the plants and animals that lived there. They often went camping in the woods. Jean learned about the plants she could eat and the habits of wild animals. She learned skills to survive in the woods.

GEORGE HAS HAD OVER 173 PETS IN HER HOME—BUT NOT AT ONE TIME! MOST OF THEM HAVE BEEN WILD ANIMALS THAT STAY FOR A WHILE AND THEN RETURN TO THE WILD.

As Jean grew older, she continued to be interested in nature. But since the third grade, she also loved to write. So after she graduated from Pennsylvania State University with a degree in science and literature, she became a reporter and wrote for many newspapers and magazines.

After marrying and having three children, George began bringing animals home for the family. Tarantulas, a raccoon, owls, robins, and many other kinds of birds were just some of the animals in their home.

"It's fascinating how many questions books inspire. Reading puts the brain to work."

A Selected Bibliography of George's Work

Luck (2006)
Charlie's Raven (2004)
Firestorm (2003)
Cliffhanger (2002)
Autumn Moon (2001)
How to Talk to Your Cat (2000)
Frightful's Mountain (1999)
Elephant Walk (1998)
Dipper of Copper Creek (1996)
There's an Owl in the Shower (1995)
The First Thanksgiving (1993)
On the Far Side of the Mountain (1990)
Shark beneath the Reef (1989)
Water Sky (1987)
One Day in the Prairie (1986)
The Talking Earth (1983)
The Wounded Wolf (1978)
Julie of the Wolves (1972)
The Summer of the Falcon (1962)
My Side of the Mountain (1959)

George's Major Literary Awards

1973 Newbery Medal
  Julie of the Wolves

1960 Newbery Honor Book
  My Side of the Mountain

"I go to these wonderful places, get to know the people, the animals, the landscape and weather, then come home to Chappaqua, New York, and write my books."

Soon, these animals became characters in George's writing.

George's children learned to enjoy nature the same way their mother had as a child. The family often went camping and hiking. These experiences in nature with her family gave George more ideas for her stories. Later, her children went into careers related to science and nature. George's visits with them continue to give her ideas and experiences for her books.

George was inspired to write the book *Julie of the Wolves* when visiting Barrow, Alaska, with her son Luke. Another visit there provided her with the information and experiences she used to write *Water Sky*. George visited another son in California to gather information for the book *There's an Owl in the Shower*.

Jean Craighead George writes about animals, plants, deserts, forests, and tundra. In her writing, she also teaches her readers about respect for the environment. They learn how people's actions can harm animals and their habitats. George's writing provides children with vivid and absorbing stories. It also provides children with important

GEORGE TRAINED A FALCON WHEN SHE WAS THIRTEEN YEARS OLD. HER BROTHERS WERE TWO OF THE FIRST FALCONERS IN THE UNITED STATES.

knowledge about their world. This knowledge helps them understand how their actions affect the environment and the world around them.

Jean Craighead George lives in Chappaqua, New York. She continues to write about the wonders of nature for young people.

❧

WHERE TO FIND OUT MORE ABOUT JEAN CRAIGHEAD GEORGE

BOOKS

Cary, Alice. *Jean Craighead George.*
Santa Barbara, Calif.: Learning Works, 1996.

Gallo, Don, ed. *Speaking for Ourselves: More Autobiographical Sketches by Notable Authors of Books for Young Adults.* Urbana, Ill.: National Council of Teachers of English, 1997.

George, Jean Craighead. *Journey Inward.*
New York: Dutton, 1982.

McElmeel, Sharron L. *100 Most Popular Children's Authors: Biographical Sketches and Bibliographies.* Englewood, Colo.: Libraries Unlimited, 1999.

Silvey, Anita, ed. *The Essential Guide to Children's Books and Their Creators.*
Boston: Houghton Mifflin Company, 2002.

WEB SITES

EDUCATIONAL PAPERBACK ASSOCIATION
http://edupaperback.org/showauth.cfm?authid=29
To read an autobiographical sketch by Jean Craighead George
and a list of her books and awards

JEAN CRAIGHEAD GEORGE'S HOME PAGE
http://www.jeancraigheadgeorge.com/
For an autobiographical sketch by Jean Craighead George, photos,
video and audio clips, a booklist, and some tips from the author on writing

---

THE BOOK *WATER SKY* INCLUDES A POLAR BEAR ATTACK. THIS REALLY HAPPENED WHEN GEORGE WAS IN AN INUIT WHALING CAMP IN NORTHERN ALASKA.

Mordicai Gerstein

Born: November 24, 1935

For Mordicai Gerstein, childhood is as real for him today as it was seventy years ago. He put his childhood love for art and books—and his childlike sense of wonder—to good use. Now his illustrations appear in more than fifty children's books. He wrote many of those books as well.

Mordicai Gerstein was born in Los Angeles, California, in 1935. Before he could walk or talk, he was drawing on the floors and walls. Encouraged by his parents, he made his first painting—a bowl of flowers—when he was four.

Mordicai also loved books. When he was four and a half, he read his first book. It was *To Think That I Saw It on Mulberry Street* by Dr. Seuss. Other favorite books were Wanda Gág's *Millions of Cats*, Lewis Carroll's *Alice in Wonderland*, and *Grimm's Fairy Tales*. Mordicai also loved comic books and cartoons, especially Bugs Bunny.

GERSTEIN DREW A WEEKLY CARTOON FOR THE *VILLAGE VOICE* NEWSPAPER DURING HIS EARLY YEARS IN NEW YORK CITY.

After high school, Gerstein attended Chouinard Art Institute in Los Angeles from 1953 to 1956. Then he went to work for United Productions of America in Burbank, California. This animation studio produced cartoons for movie theaters.

> *"For me, picture books are little theaters one holds in the hand and operates by turning the pages."*

In 1957, Gerstein married artist Sandra MacDonald. They eventually had two sons, Jesse and Aram. The couple moved to New York City, where Gerstein created animated films and TV commercials. At night, he worked on his own paintings.

Gerstein met children's book author Elizabeth Levy in 1970. She invited him to illustrate her mystery book *Something Queer Is Going On*, which came out in 1973. It was the first in a multibook series about two friends, Gwen and Jill. Gerstein and Levy went on to produce the Fletcher series, featuring Jill's dog, Fletcher.

> *"I'm still in touch with my childhood. Most writers of children's books, as well as artists and painters, say the same. . . . I believe childhood is the well we draw upon—it is the source of everything."*

From the moment he illustrated *Something Queer Is Going On*, Gerstein was excited about creating picture books. In the early 1980s, he abandoned animation and began

GERSTEIN OFTEN RIDES HIS BICYCLE FROM HIS HOME TO HIS STUDIO.

A Selected Bibliography of Gerstein's Work

Learning to Fly (2007)

White Ram: A Tale of Rosh Hashanah Based on Jewish Legends (2006)

The Old Country (2005)

Sholom's Treasure (Illustrations only, 2004)

The Man Who Walked between the Towers (2003)

A Hare-Raising Tail (Illustrations only, 2002)

What Charlie Heard (2002)

Queen Esther, the Morning Star (2000)

Victor (1998)

The Wild Boy (1998)

The Shadow of a Flying Bird: A Legend of the Kurdistani Jews (1994)

The Mountains of Tibet (1987)

The Seal Mother (1986)

Tales of Pan (1986)

Arnold of the Ducks (1983)

Something Queer Is Going On (Illustrations only, 1973)

Gerstein's Major Literary Awards

2004 Boston Globe-Horn Book Picture Book Award
2004 Caldecott Medal
   The Man Who Walked between the Towers

writing his own stories. In 1983, *Arnold of the Ducks*—the first book he wrote and illustrated—was published.

Gerstein left New York City in 1983 and moved to Northampton, Massachusetts. His first marriage had ended in divorce, and in 1984, he married illustrator Susan Harris. They had a daughter, Risa. Meanwhile, Gerstein continued to illustrate others' books, as well as to write and illustrate more than thirty books of his own. They included Bible stories, mythology, biographies, and alphabet books.

Although many of Gerstein's subjects are humorous, others are serious and thought-provoking. Two books—*The Wild Boy* and *Victor*—are about a boy in France who was found in 1800 living in the wild. He was never able to fit in to civilized society. *The Man Who Walked between the Towers* is about Frenchman Philippe Petit, who walked across a tightrope between New York City's World Trade Center towers in 1974. Those towers were destroyed in the 2001 terrorist attack. For Gerstein, the book, which was published in 2003, was a way of responding to the attack and celebrating the human spirit.

❧

WHERE TO FIND OUT MORE ABOUT MORDICAI GERSTEIN

BOOK
Ward, Martha E. *Authors of Books for Young People.* 3rd ed. Metuchen, N.J.: Scarecrow Press, 1990.

WEB SITES
THE HORN BOOK
http://www.hbook.com/publications/magazine/articles/jul04_gordon.asp
For an article about Gerstein by a former editor

MORDICAI GERSTEIN
http://www.mordicaigerstein.com/
For the author's biography

PBS HOME
http://www.pbs.org/newshour/bb/entertainment/jan-june04/towers_02-16.html
For a transcript of an interview with Gerstein

SEVEN PUBLISHERS REJECTED *ARNOLD OF THE DUCKS* BEFORE IT WAS ACCEPTED FOR PUBLICATION.

Gail Gibbons

Born: August 1, 1944

G ail Gibbons writes and illustrates her own books. She paints with bright, bold, beautiful colors and writes with simple, colorful words. Since 1975, Gibbons has written and illustrated more than 100 books for children from preschool to fifth grade. Mostly nonfiction, her books are filled with interesting facts and creative ideas.

She was born on August 1, 1944, in Oak Park, Illinois. Gail was a curious child and became interested in drawing at an early age. A kindergarten teacher recognized the young girl's talent and convinced her parents to pay for art lessons.

After graduating from high school, she studied graphic design at the University of Illinois, where she met Glenn Gibbons. They married

---

GAIL GIBBONS PUT TOGETHER HER FIRST BOOK WHEN SHE WAS FOUR YEARS OLD. SHE USED YARN TO BIND THE PAGES TOGETHER.

in 1966. The next year she graduated with a degree in fine arts and began working as a graphic artist for WCIA, a local television station in Champaign, Illinois.

In 1970, Gibbons and her husband moved to New York City, where she did artwork for a children's television program on NBC called *Take a Giant Step.* Inspired by children on the show, Gibbons decided to try her hand at writing and illustrating her own stories. It took her five years to accomplish her goal.

In 1972, Gibbons's husband died tragically in an accident. Gibbons began working on NBC's nightly news

"The type of books I write are nonfiction books. This is because I love researching so much. I get to ask lots of questions, just like when I was a kid. I also get to travel and meet lots of interesting people."

program. She continued to write and illustrate on the side. In 1975, she published her first book, *Willy and His Wheel Wagon,* which deals with math.

A year later, Gibbons married Kent Ancliffe, a builder, and became stepmother to his two children. They built a home in Corinth, Vermont, where the family now lives. Gibbons spends most of the year at their quaint Vermont farmhouse, writing and illustrating books and helping her husband run their maple syrup business.

IN 1982, GIBBONS EARNED A CERTIFICATE OF APPRECIATION FROM THE U.S. POSTMASTER GENERAL FOR *THE POST OFFICE BOOK: MAIL AND HOW IT MOVES.*

A Selected Bibliography of Gibbons's Work

Groundhog Day! Shadow or No Shadow? (2007)

Vegetable Book (2006)

Dinosaur Discoveries (2005)

Quilting Bee (2004)

The Berries Book (2002)

Giant Pandas (2002)

Behold—The Unicorns! (2001)

Ducks! (2001)

Marshes & Swamps (1998)

Soaring with the Wind: The Bald Eagle (1998)

Click! A Book about Cameras and Taking Pictures (1997)

Cats (1996)

Christmas on an Island (1994)

Nature's Green Umbrella: Tropical Rain Forests (1994)

Spiders (1993)

Surrounded by Sea: Life on a New England Fishing Island (1991)

Weather Words and What They Mean (1990)

Monarch Butterfly (1989)

Trains (1987)

From Path to Highway: The Story of the Boston Post Road (1986)

Check It Out! The Book about Libraries (1985)

The Milk Makers (1985)

The Seasons of Arnold's Apple Tree (1984)

Cars and How They Go (Illustrations only, 1983)

The Post Office Book: Mail and How It Moves (1982)

The Missing Maple Syrup Sap Mystery; or, How Maple Syrup Is Made (1979)

Willy and His Wheel Wagon (1975)

Ever curious about the world around her, Gibbons writes about what she sees. Often, she explores what is at hand. She has written about the maple syrup business (*The Missing Maple Syrup Sap Mystery; or, How Maple Syrup Is Made*) and their second home on an island in Maine (*Surrounded by Sea: Life on a New England Fishing Island*). Frequent visits to a nearby dairy farm led her to write *The Milk Makers.* And visits to bald eagle nesting sites prompted her to write *Soaring with the Wind: The Bald Eagle.*

Sometimes, her research has taken her to distant places. Once she visited the Florida Everglades to gather information for her book called *Marshes & Swamps.*

Another time she toured the islands of Saba and Dominica to do research for the book *Nature's Green Umbrella: Tropical Rain Forests.*

Over the years, Gibbons's books have won many awards. Perhaps the award she cherishes most is the one she receives each time a child reads one of her books and answers the questions Gibbons asked herself before beginning to write: Who lives there? How does that work? Why does that happen? What can I do to have fun?

"To me, putting a nonfiction book together is like watching the pieces of a puzzle finally fitting together."

WHERE TO FIND OUT MORE ABOUT GAIL GIBBONS

BOOKS

Kovacs, Deborah, and James Preller. *Meet the Authors and Illustrators: 60 Creators of Favorite Children's Books Talk about Their Work.* Vol. 2. New York: Scholastic, 1993.

McElmeel, Sharron L. *100 Most Popular Picture Book Authors and Illustrators: Biographical Sketches and Bibliographies.* Englewood, Colo.: Libraries Unlimited, 2000.

WEB SITES

EDUCATIONAL PAPERBACK ASSOCIATION
http://edupaperback.org/showauth.cfm?authid=240
To read a biographical sketch of and a booklist for Gail Gibbons

GAIL GIBBONS HOME PAGE
http://www.gailgibbons.com/
To read an autobiographical sketch by Gail Gibbons and a booklist

GIBBONS AND HER HUSBAND HAVE A LITTLE FARMHOUSE ON AN ISLAND OFF THE COAST OF MAINE. GIBBONS'S BOOK *CHRISTMAS ON AN ISLAND* IS SET THERE.

James Cross Giblin

Born: July 8, 1933

He has written a book about windows and a book about milk. He has written books about dinosaur bones and human diseases. And the list goes on. James Cross Giblin writes nonfiction books for children. He has written books on a wide range of topics and people.

He has been working as a writer for more than forty-five years. His best-known books include *Chimney Sweeps: Yesterday and Today, The Truth about Santa Claus, Walls: Defenses throughout History,* and *The Amazing Life of Benjamin Franklin.*

James Cross Giblin was born on July 8, 1933, in

GIBLIN HAS WRITTEN A BOOK CALLED *WRITING BOOKS FOR YOUNG PEOPLE.* THIS BOOK HELPS ADULTS WRITE CHILDREN'S BOOKS.

The Amazing Life of
BENJAMIN FRANKLIN

by JAMES CROSS GIBLIN • illustrated by MICHAEL DOOLING

Cleveland, Ohio. He grew up in a small town near Cleveland.

As a young boy, James was very shy. He enjoyed reading books and drawing. He read the comic strips in the newspaper and drew his own comic strips. He would draw the pictures, and then his mother would print the words on the strips. He filled many sketchbooks with his comic strips and other drawings.

James also enjoyed going to the movies. He was especially

A Selected Bibliography of Giblin's Work

Good Brother, Bad Brother: The Story of Edwin Booth and John Wilkes Booth (2005)

Secrets of the Sphinx (2004)

Life and Death of Adolf Hitler (2002)

The Amazing Life of Benjamin Franklin (2000)

The Century That Was: Reflections on the Last One Hundred Years (2000)

The Mystery of the Mammoth Bones: And How It Was Solved (1999)

Charles A. Lindbergh: A Human Hero (1997)

The Dwarf, the Giant, and the Unicorn: A Tale of King Arthur (1996)

When Plague Strikes: The Black Death, Smallpox, AIDS (1995)

Thomas Jefferson: A Picture Book Biography (1994)

Be Seated: A Book about Chairs (1993)

Edith Wilson: The Woman Who Ran the United States (1992)

George Washington: A Picture Book Biography (1992)

The Truth about Unicorns (1991)

The Riddle of the Rosetta Stone: Key to Ancient Egypt (1990)

Let There Be Light: A Book about Windows (1988)

From Hand to Mouth, or, How We Invented Knives, Forks, Spoons, Chopsticks, and the Table Manners to Go with Them (1987)

Milk: The Fight for Purity (1986)

The Truth about Santa Claus (1985)

Walls: Defenses throughout History (1984)

Fireworks, Picnics, and Flags (1983)

Chimney Sweeps: Yesterday and Today (1982)

The Skyscraper Book (1981)

The Scarecrow Book (1980)

Giblin's Major Literary Awards

2005 Boston Globe–Horn Book Nonfiction Honor Book
Good Brother, Bad Brother: The Story of Edwin Booth and John Wilkes Booth

2005 Orbis Pictus Honor Book
Secrets of the Sphinx

2001 Orbis Pictus Honor Book
The Amazing Life of Benjamin Franklin

1998 Orbis Pictus Honor Book
Charles A. Lindbergh: A Human Hero

1986 Boston Globe–Horn Book Nonfiction Honor Book
The Truth about Santa Claus

1983 American Book Award
Chimney Sweeps: Yesterday and Today

interested in spy films and movies
about World War II (1939–1945).

> *"I love research. . . . I enjoy making things clear for readers."*

When James Giblin was in junior
high school, he began working on the
school newspaper. He was not sure he wanted to work on the paper, but
his teacher encouraged him to get involved. James discovered that he
loved coming up with ideas for stories and pictures for the paper.

In high school, James got involved in school plays. Though he
was still very shy, he found that he could reveal his feelings when he
was onstage.

Giblin's interest in drama continued in college. He starred in many
theater productions as a college student. He even won a contest to appear
on a radio drama with a professional actress. Then his interest shifted to
directing and writing plays. His first play was written and performed in

> *"I try to write books that I would have enjoyed reading when I was the age of my readers."*

1954. In 1955, Giblin earned a master's degree
in fine arts from Columbia University.

By 1959, Giblin needed to find a career
that was more stable than theater. He took
a job as an editor for a publishing company.
The new position gave him the chance
to read and edit books written by other

GIBLIN ENJOYED READING THE COMIC STRIP *BLONDIE* WHEN HE WAS GROWING UP.

138

authors. He worked in publishing for more than twenty years before he began writing his own books.

Giblin's first book, *The Scarecrow Book,* was published in 1980. Since that time, he has written more than twenty nonfiction books for young people. Many people like Giblin's books because he is able to write about complex things in a way that is easy to understand.

James Cross Giblin has won many awards for his nonfiction books. He lives in New York City, where he continues to write books for young people.

❧

WHERE TO FIND OUT MORE ABOUT JAMES CROSS GIBLIN

BOOKS

Children's Literature Review, Vol. 29. Detroit: Gale, 1993.

Silvey, Anita, ed. *The Essential Guide to Children's Books and Their Creators.* Boston: Houghton Mifflin Company, 2002.

WEB SITES

CHILDREN'S BOOK COUNCIL
http://www.cbcbooks.org/cbcmagazine/meet/giblin_james_cross.html
For an article about the author

OHIO READING ROAD TRIP
http://www.ohioreadingroadtrip.org/giblin/
For a biographical sketch of the author.

UNIVERSITY OF SOUTHERN MISSISSIPPI DE GRUMMOND COLLECTION
http://www.lib.usm.edu/~degrum/findaids/giblin.htm
To read a biographical sketch of and a booklist for James Cross Giblin

———

JAMES CROSS GIBLIN HAS WRITTEN ARTICLES AND STORIES FOR *COBBLESTONE, HIGHLIGHTS FOR CHILDREN,* AND *CRICKET.*

Patricia Reilly Giff

Born: April 26, 1935

s a young girl, Patricia Reilly Giff dreamed of being a writer. Before becoming a writer, she worked as a teacher and reading consultant for many years. She eventually achieved her dream of writing books for children and young people. She has written dozens of books, including the Kids of the Polk Street School series; the Polka Dot, Private Eye series; and the Ballet Slippers series.

Patricia Reilly Giff was born on April 26, 1935, in Brooklyn, New York. When she was growing up, she almost always had a book in her hands. Her friends would get together and play games in the park. Patricia would sit under a tree and read. She also loved to sit

---

GIFF OWNS A CHILDREN'S BOOKSTORE IN FAIRFIELD, CONNECTICUT, CALLED THE DINOSAUR'S PAW.

with her father and mother and have them read to her.

Patricia often borrowed books from the library. Over the years, she read all the books for children and young people that were in the library. She almost ran out of books to read. But the librarian found books for her from the adult section.

> *"I spent most of my childhood with a book in my hands. I read before the sun was up, then hunched over the breakfast table with my book in my lap. After school, I'd sit in the kitchen leaning against the warm radiator dreaming over a story."*

When she finished high school, Giff attended Marymount College in New York. She knew she wanted to be a writer, so she decided to study English. She changed her mind after she read books by famous writers. She did not think she was talented enough to be a writer. She studied history instead.

After Giff finished college, she became a teacher in the New York City public schools. She got her first teaching job in 1956.

Giff was married in 1959. By the time she was forty years old, she had three children and was a reading teacher in a public school. She realized that she had not done any writing.

Since Giff still wanted to be a writer, she decided to start working on a book. "I dragged myself out of bed in the early morning darkness

---

GIFF HAS THREE CATS NAMED J. R. FIDDLE, BONNIE, AND JAKE.

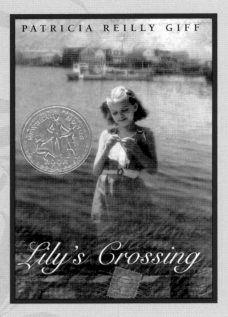

A Selected Bibliography of Giff's Work

Water Street (2006)
Willow Run (2005)
House of Tailors (2004)
Maggie's Door (2003)
Pictures of Hollis Woods (2002)
All the Way Home (2001)
Nory Ryan's Song (2000)
Adiós, Anna (1998)
A Glass Slipper for Rosie (1997)
Lily's Crossing (1997)
Dance with Rosie (1996)
Ronald Morgan Goes to Camp (1995)
Ronald Morgan Goes to Bat (1988)
Watch Out, Ronald Morgan! (1985)
The Almost Awful Play (1984)
The Gift of the Pirate Queen (1982)
The Winter Worm Business (1981)
Today Was a Terrible Day (1980)
Fourth-Grade Celebrity (1979)

Giff's Major Literary Awards

2003 Newbery Honor Book
  Pictures of Hollis Woods

1998 Newbery Honor Book
1997 Boston Globe–Horn Book Fiction Honor Book
  Lily's Crossing

to spend an hour or two at my typewriter before I had to leave for school," Giff notes. It took her several years to finish her first children's book. The book, *Fourth-Grade Celebrity,* was published in 1979. Giff then decided that she would follow her dream of becoming a writer.

Most of Giff's books are written for students in the middle grades. She writes novels and has created several book series. Her books are known for their humor and familiar situations.

"Anyone who laughs and cries, anyone who feels, can write. It's only talking on paper . . . talking about things that matter to us."

Patricia Reilly Giff lives in Connecticut with her husband. This productive author continues to write books for children and young people.

❧

WHERE TO FIND OUT MORE ABOUT PATRICIA REILLY GIFF

BOOKS

Holtze, Sally Holmes, ed. *Fifth Book of Junior Authors & Illustrators.* New York: H. W. Wilson Company, 1983.

Kovacs, Deborah, and James Preller. *Meet the Authors and Illustrators: 60 Creators of Favorite Children's Books Talk about Their Work.* Vol. 2. New York: Scholastic, 1993.

McElmeel, Sharron L. *100 Most Popular Picture Book Authors and Illustrators: Biographical Sketches and Bibliographies.* Englewood, Colo.: Libraries Unlimited, 2000.

WEB SITES

EDUCATIONAL PAPERBACK ASSOCIATION
http://edupaperback.org/showauth.cfm?authid=30
To read an autobiographical sketch by and a booklist for Patricia Reilly Giff

RANDOM HOUSE: AUTHORS/ILLUSTRATORS
http://www.randomhouse.com/features/patriciareillygiff/
To read a biographical sketch of Patricia Reilly Giff

SOME OF GIFF'S FAVORITE CHILDHOOD BOOKS WERE *LITTLE WOMEN, THE SECRET GARDEN,* THE BLACK STALLION SERIES, AND THE NANCY DREW SERIES.

Paul Goble

Born: September 27, 1933

Paul Goble writes and illustrates books about Native American life. But he grew up thousands of miles away from North America.

Paul Goble was born on September 27, 1933, in Surrey, England. As a child, he was fascinated by the lives of American Indians. As Paul grew

older, he longed to know more about their spirituality, stories, and way of life.

Paul Goble studied art at the Central School of Arts and Crafts in London. After he graduated, he stayed in London to work, teaching art and designing furniture.

In 1959, Goble had a chance to visit the United States. Back in England in 1969, he published

IN 1959, PAUL GOBLE BECAME A MEMBER OF THE YAKIMA AND THE SIOUX TRIBES. HIS AMERICAN INDIAN NAME IS LITTLE THUNDER.

his first book for children. *Red Hawk's Account of Custer's Last Battle* told the story of a battle between Native Americans and the U.S. Army from the Native American point of view.

In 1977, Goble moved to the United States. He was thrilled to have the chance to live, work, and talk with Native Americans. In 1984, he became a U.S. citizen. After living for a while in Nebraska, he settled in South Dakota.

Goble's books are mainly about Native Americans of the plains. He writes and illustrates stories about the Lakota, the Cheyenne, and the Blackfoot. Goble researches stories that have been told and retold for generations. Then he writes

THE GIRL WHO LOVED WILD HORSES
by PAUL GOBLE

A Selected Bibliography of Goble's Work

All Our Relatives: Traditional Native American Thoughts About Nature (2005)

Song of Creation (2004)

Mystic Horse (2002)

Storm Maker's Tipi (2001)

Iktomi Loses His Eyes: A Plains Indian Story (1999)

Iktomi and the Coyote: A Plains Indian Story (1998)

Adopted by the Eagles: A Plains Indians Story of Friendship and Treachery (1994)

Crow Chief: A Plains Indian Story (1992)

Love Flute: Story and Illustrations (1992)

I Sing for the Animals (1991)

Dream Wolf (1990)

Her Seven Brothers (1988)

Iktomi and the Boulder: A Plains Indian Story (1988)

Death of the Iron Horse (1987)

The Great Race of the Birds and Animals (1985)

The Legend of the White Buffalo Woman (1984)

Star Boy (1983)

The Gift of the Sacred Dog: Story and Illustrations (1980)

The Girl Who Loved Wild Horses (1978)

Red Hawk's Account of Custer's Last Battle: The Battle of the Little Bighorn, 25 June 1876 (1969)

Goble's Major Literary Award

1979 Caldecott Medal
The Girl Who Loved Wild Horses

> *"I feel that I have seen and learned many wonderful things from Indian people which most people would never have the opportunity to experience. I simply wanted to express and to share these things which I love so much."*

them for children and adds brilliant illustrations.

Goble's pictures often show Native Americans doing everyday tasks or joining in celebrations. They pick berries, make clothing, and gather for dances. Some pictures show beautiful scenes from nature. These pictures often have dozens of small animals or plants in them. At times, Goble paints using bold patterns and silhouettes. Sometimes he uses rich colors and sometimes only earth tones.

Many of Goble's stories are amusing, but they teach serious lessons. They teach children not to be greedy, sneaky, lazy, or dishonest. Other stories show the importance of respecting people, animals, and the environment. Often his characters are animals that can speak or that understand humans.

One of Goble's favorite characters is Iktomi. Iktomi uses tricks to try to get his way. At times, the character appears as a spider. In the Iktomi stories, the trickster is often outsmarted by some other character,

---

GOBLE'S BOOKS HAVE BEEN CHOSEN FOR THE
LIBRARY OF CONGRESS CHILDREN'S BOOK OF THE YEAR AWARD.

and his plans backfire. The Iktomi stories are most enjoyable when told by a storyteller. The storyteller often asks the listeners questions, trying to lead them deeper into the story.

Although he is himself not an American Indian, Paul Goble has won the respect of many Native Americans. Some of his books have even been used in schools on Lakota reservations to help educate children about their culture.

WHERE TO FIND OUT MORE ABOUT PAUL GOBLE

BOOKS

Kovacs, Deborah, and James Preller. *Meet the Authors and Illustrators: 60 Creators of Favorite Children's Books Talk about Their Work.* Vol. 2. New York: Scholastic, 1993.

McElmeel, Sharron L. *100 Most Popular Picture Book Authors and Illustrators: Biographical Sketches and Bibliographies.* Englewood, Colo.: Libraries Unlimited, 2000.

Silvey, Anita, ed. *The Essential Guide to Children's Books and Their Creators.* Boston: Houghton Mifflin Company, 2002.

WEB SITES

INTERVIEW WITH GOBLE
http://www.eerdmans.com/gobleinterview.htm
This site contains an interview with the author.

UNIVERSITY OF NEBRASKA: PAUL GOBLE
http://monet.unk.edu/mona/exhibit/artists/goble/gobleexh.html
To read a biographical sketch of Paul Goble

GOBLE RESEARCHES THE CLOTHING OF NATIVE AMERICAN TRIBES SO HE CAN SHOW IT ACCURATELY IN HIS PAINTINGS.

Kenneth Grahame

Born: March 8, 1859
Died: July 6, 1932

enneth Grahame is best known for his beloved children's classic *The Wind in the Willows*. Grahame claimed that he most liked writing for children ages four to seven. But for Grahame, those childhood years were anything but happy.

Kenneth Grahame was born in Edinburgh, Scotland, in 1859. The Grahame children—three boys and a girl—spent their early years in Scotland's western Highlands. Their mother died of scarlet fever just before Kenneth turned five.

Kenneth's father, an alcoholic, was unable to raise the children, so he turned them over to their grandmother. She lived in the countryside village of Cookham Dene in southern England. Kenneth missed his parents terribly. His grandmother did not pay much attention to

U.S. PRESIDENT THEODORE ROOSEVELT ADMIRED GRAHAME'S WRITINGS. AFTER *THE WIND IN THE WILLOWS* WAS PUBLISHED IN ENGLAND, ROOSEVELT ARRANGED FOR IT TO BE PUBLISHED IN THE UNITED STATES.

the children, so he often roamed the countryside, lost in daydreams.

When Kenneth was nine, he was sent away to Saint Edward's School, a boarding school in Oxford, England. After finishing there in 1875, he hoped to go on to Oxford University,

> *"A sentence that is easy to read may have been difficult to put together. . . . Writing is not easy. . . . It is, at its best, a pleasurable agony."*

but the family could not afford it. In 1878, at age nineteen, he began working as a clerk at the Bank of England in London.

Grahame found his bank job boring, so on the side, he began writing stories for British journals. They were collected and published as *The Pagan Papers* in 1893. Grahame's next book was *The Golden Age*, a collection of stories about orphaned children and their adventures. Grahame continued to write about these children in *Dream Days*. Grahame became secretary of the bank in 1898 and married Elspeth Thomson in 1899. Unlike Grahame, she was rather snobbish, and their marriage was not a happy one. Their son, Alistair, arrived in 1900. He was born blind in one eye and with a squint in the other eye, and his parents nicknamed him Mouse.

Alistair was spoiled and often threw tantrums. On Alistair's fourth birthday, Grahame began telling him tales about Mole, Rat,

---

GRAHAME'S GRANDMOTHER'S HOUSE AND GARDEN BY THE THAMES RIVER IN COOKHAM DENE WAS THE SETTING FOR *THE WIND IN THE WILLOWS*.

A Selected Bibliography of Grahame's Work

The Wind in the Willows (1908)
Dream Days (1898)
The Golden Age (1895)
Pagan Papers (1893)

Badger, Toad, and other animals in the Wild Wood to calm him during a crying fit. Even when Alistair was away from home, Grahame wrote the boy letters with more of the animals' escapades. The letters typically began, "My dearest Mouse, No doubt you will be interested to hear the further adventures. . . ." Those tales were collected and published as *The Wind in the Willows* in 1908.

> *"[Children's] readiness to welcome a perfect miracle at any hour of the day or night, is a thing more precious than any of the labored acquisitions of adult mankind."*

The book was a great success. After it was published, Grahame retired from the bank and lived quietly.

A terrible tragedy struck in 1920. Alistair, a student at Oxford University, had been suffering from depression. Just before his twentieth birthday, he ended his life by lying on the tracks in front of an oncoming train. After the incident, Grahame said, "I doubt very much if I shall ever write another book." True to his word, he did not.

In 1924, Grahame and his wife moved to the village of Pangbourne, alongside the Thames River in southern England. He died there in 1932 at the age of seventy-three.

❧

WHERE TO FIND OUT MORE ABOUT KENNETH GRAHAME

BOOKS

Dictionary of Literary Biography, British Fantasy and Science-Fiction Writers Before World War I. Detroit: Gale, 1997.

Silvey, Anita, ed. *The Essential Guide to Children's Books and Their Creators*. Boston: Houghton Mifflin Company, 2002.

Sutherland, Zena. *Children & Books*. 9th ed. Boston: Allyn & Bacon, 1997.

Twentieth-Century Literary Criticism. Vol. 64. Detroit: Gale, 1996.

WEB SITE

CLASSIC READER
http://www.classicreader.com/author.php/aut.48/
To read a biography of Grahame

———

GRAHAME SERVED AS EDITOR FOR *THE CAMBRIDGE BOOK OF POETRY FOR CHILDREN*, PUBLISHED IN **1916**.

Eloise Greenfield

Born: May 17, 1929

Eloise Greenfield offers a wealth of reading experiences for African American children. She is the author of more than forty books, ranging from picture books to poetry to biographies. In each book, she portrays the warmth of loving families and communities.

Eloise Greenfield was born Eloise Little in 1929 in Parmele, North Carolina. When she was a baby, the family moved to Washington, D.C., the nation's capital. Eloise was an early reader, and she was an excellent student. She was painfully shy, though, and avoided answering questions in class.

When Eloise was nine, the family moved to Langston Terrace, a housing project in Washington, D.C. Eloise enjoyed her time there. She was surrounded by neighbors who were friendly and helpful to one another. The local library was a short walk away, and Eloise was a regular visitor there. Music was another happy part of her life. Her family had a piano, and she took piano lessons until she was sixteen.

GREENFIELD HAS TAUGHT CREATIVE WRITING TO ELEMENTARY AND JUNIOR HIGH SCHOOL STUDENTS.

Eloise attended Cardozo High School in Washington, D.C., and graduated in 1946. She enrolled in the city's Miner Teachers College, hoping to become an elementary school teacher. However, because she was so shy, it was hard for her to present the required teaching demonstrations. She dropped out in 1949 and went to work as a clerk-typist in the U.S. Patent Office. The next year, she married Robert Greenfield, whom she had known since she was thirteen. They later had two children, Steven and Monica.

In her spare time, Greenfield wrote poems, songs, and short stories. In 1962, she was proud to see her poem "To a Violin" published in the *Hartford*

A Selected Bibliography of Greenfield's Work

When the Horses Ride By (2006)

In the Land of Words (2004)

I Can Draw a Weeposaur and Other Dinosaurs (2001)

For the Love of the Game: Michael Jordan and Me (1997)

Kia Tanisha (1997)

Talk about a Family (1993)

My Daddy and I (1991)

Night on Neighborhood Street (1991)

Nathaniel Talking (1988)

Alesia (1981)

Daydreamers (1981)

Darlene (1980)

Childtimes: A Three-Generation Memoir (with Lessie Jones Little, 1979)

Honey, I Love, and Other Love Poems (1978)

I Can Do It by Myself (1978)

Africa Dream (1977)

Me and Neesie (1975)

Paul Robeson (1975)

She Come Bringing Me That Little Baby Girl (1974)

Rosa Parks (1973)

Bubbles (1972)

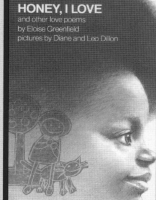

HONEY, I LOVE
and other love poems
by Eloise Greenfield
pictures by Diane and Leo Dillon

Greenfield's Major Literary Awards

1992 Coretta Scott King Author Honor Book
Night on Neighborhood Street

1990 Coretta Scott King Author Honor Book
Nathaniel Talking

1980 Boston Globe-Horn Book Nonfiction Honor Book
1980 Coretta Scott King Author Honor Book
Childtimes: A Three-Generation Memoir

1978 Coretta Scott King Author Award
Africa Dream

1978 Coretta Scott King Author Honor Book
Mary McCleod Bethune

1975 Boston Globe-Horn Book Picture Book Honor Book
She Come Bringing Me That Little Baby Girl

1974 Carter G. Woodson Book Award
Rosa Parks

> *"I want to . . . choose and order words that children will want to celebrate. I want to make them shout and laugh and blink back tears and care about themselves."*

Times of Hartford, Connecticut. Greenfield began reading books about how to write and sell stories. She also joined the District of Columbia Black Writers' Workshop in 1971. This group encouraged the writing and publishing of African American literature.

In 1972, Greenfield's picture book *Bubbles* was published. Inspired by her success, she went on to write more picture books, poetry books, board books for young children, young-adult novels, and biographies of famous African Americans. These biographies offer positive, inspiring images of figures such as actor Paul Robeson, educator Mary McLeod Bethune, and basketball star Michael Jordan.

Greenfield's books often reflect the kind of environment she knew as a child. They portray loving, supportive African American families and neighborhoods. Many of her stories focus on difficult family issues. In *She Come Bringing Me That Little Baby Girl*, a boy at first resents his new baby sister but comes to treasure her. In *Talk about a Family*, a girl adjusts to her parents' separation.

The sounds and rhythms of language have always fascinated Greenfield. So it's no surprise that poetry is one of her strengths. She likes to create what she calls "word madness"—the readers' joyous reaction to

Childtimes: A Three-Generation Memoir brings together the lifetime memories of Greenfield, her mother, and her grandmother.

the words on the page. The poetry collection *Nathaniel Talking* explores the language rhythms of a boy's family members, including Nathaniel's own rap style.

Eloise Greenfield still lives and works in Washington, D.C.

> "*Hope is part of human nature when people are not too beaten down. It's critical that you have someone around to reflect hope . . . both for children and for adults.*"

WHERE TO FIND OUT MORE ABOUT ELOISE GREENFIELD

BOOKS

Contemporary Black Biography. Vol. 9. Detroit: Gale, 1995.

Kovacs, Deborah, and James Preller. *Meet the Authors and Illustrators*. Vol. 2. New York: Scholastic, 1993.

Pendergast, Sara, and Tom Pendergast, eds. *St. James Guide to Children's Writers*. 5th ed. Detroit: St. James Press, 1999.

Sutherland, Zena. *Children & Books*. 9th ed. Boston: Allyn & Bacon, 1997.

WEB SITES

HARPERCOLLINS
http://www.harperchildrens.com/authorintro/index.asp?authorid=12162
For a biography, a list of books, and an interview with the author

HOUGHTON MIFFLIN MEET THE AUTHOR
http://www.eduplace.com/kids/hmr/mtai/greenfield.html
For a brief a biography of the author

MOST OF GREENFIELD'S PICTURE BOOKS ARE ILLUSTRATED BY JAN SPIVEY GILCHRIST.

INDEX